Planting the Faith...

A History of St. John's Episcopal Church
Memphis, Tennessee

Mission Statement

To become so filled with the Spirit of God
that the light of Christ will shine through us and
inspire others to glorify our Father in heaven.

Planting the Faith...

A History of St. John's Episcopal Church
Memphis, Tennessee

by

Betty B. Larkey

Book design by Virginia Donelson Curry

Production by Gloria C. White & Associates

Proofreading by David Yawn

Vestry Committee for Church History:

James F. Russell, Esq., Chairman

Sarah Loaring-Clark Flowers

Mrs. Hal P. Bailey, Jr.

Mrs. Haywood Henderson

©1996 St. John's Episcopal Church

Memphis, Tennessee

All rights reserved.

Library of Congress: 96-70465

ISBN: 0-9654666-0-4

Printed in the United States of America by:

Starr-Toof

670 S. Cooper St., Memphis, TN 38104

Contents

Bishop's Foreword

What St. John's Means to Me

It is a great privilege to have served St. John's. When we came here, it was a homecoming: to hometown, to family, friends and a return to the city where I was ordained deacon and priest.

My ministry was simply another tier on the building of ministry which preceded me in St. John's distinguished history. Tib Loaring-Clark left his legacy of scholarship and a magnificent new building and murals. Wallace Pennepacker's hallmarks of unwavering ethical standards and theological wisdom presented unequivocally the message of resurrection and redemption. Stewart Wood brought change and an outward look at the social action needs of the larger community.

I knew we needed, and we began, work on our buildings, grounds and programs, but most important was the need to be knit together, to trust one another, to get over disputes and move ahead. We worked together, saw many projects completed, had fun, and through the grace of God became a family again.

Throughout my ministry I have had giants in the faith to show me the way. Many of them are at St. John's.

James M. Coleman

James M. Coleman
Bishop of West Tennessee

Dedication

This history is in praise of the glory of God and in memory of devoted parishoners through 15 decades of change. It is a tribute to the three men whose long tenure was most influential in mapping the unknown for St. John's community of faithful believers:

Alfred Loaring-Clark, first Rector

Wallace Pennepacker, who succeeded him

Richard White, organist for 36 years

Acknowledgements

This history was begun almost 20 years ago by Mrs. Wallace Pennepacker (Frances), who organized 25 teams to interview more than 100 parishioners, providing invaluable oral history for the project. Unfortunately, she was unable to continue the project and records she accumulated remained in boxes until the project was re-inaugurated in mid-1995.

The project is funded by a gracious gift by Mrs. James D. Robinson.

To the many generous parishioners, both present and former, who graciously contributed photographs, facts, stories, and support—thanks! The project would not have been possible otherwise. Hud Andrews contributed photographs. Art Mayhall researched trust deeds. Claire Ashley, Sallie Fox, and Mimi Smith compiled the list of Vestrymen. Generous help was also given by the staff of the History Department of Memphis & Shelby County Public Library. Dr. Franklin Wright, Susan Miles, Dot Work, Ana Daggett, and Annie Armour-Jones gave invaluable research help in the archives of St. Mary's Cathedral and at Sewanee. John Allen and the staff at St. John's provided records and facts. A large committee of parishioners including Frances and Ed Newell, Tom Mitchell, Richard and Mahaffey White, and Bill Murray, read copy, made corrections, and gave support. Lee and Nancy Wakeman, former parishioners of St. John's, loaned books from the library at Calvary. Virginia Curry, Gloria White, and David Yawn made the critical decisions of design, production, and proofing that make it a book to treasure.

The Vestry Committee for the Church History deserves special thanks for all their time and encouragement given to this project. It wouldn't have happened without Jim Russell, Chairman, who organized, telephoned, arranged meetings, read copy, and most generously supported every aspect of accomplishing this tribute to all the people who made St. John's a lighthouse.

And, finally, to The Rev. Mr. Alfred Loaring-Clark for his writings of 50 years ago, quoted quite liberally because of their relevance today.

Beginnings

1

$\mathcal{L}$ike a good mystery, the history of St. John's Episcopal Church in Shelby County, Tennessee, leaves clues without solutions. Just as the avid researcher, stumbling toward substantiation, discovers a small fact, another tantalizing clue also emerges.

Churches, like other living, growing bodies, have genealogy. Episcopal churches usually have well-documented lineage. Birth, nurture, milestones faithfully recorded in parish records. For St. John's Parish, however, history is veiled in smoke, with old records lost by fire. What is known parallels the turbulence of Memphis' history.

Nearly 300 years after Hernando DeSoto traveled along the Chickasaw Bluffs and discovered the Mississippi River for the second time, a little Indian camp on the southernmost of the four bluffs became the city of Memphis. Although historians credited DeSoto with discovering the Mississippi on his 1541 journey looking for gold, European cartographers knew of the river by the beginning of the 16th century. But 66 years before the founding of Jamestown, when DeSoto's men camped on the bluff before crossing the river into Arkansas, few white men had ever seen the area.

It was more than a century later that the first white settlers came to the site, in 1673. It was another century and a half before the town began.

The bluffs were inhabited by the Chickasaw Indians, agricultural and hunting people who roamed all of the Western Territory as hunting ground. The Chickasaws were among the tribes later called the "Five Civilized Nations." When DeSoto's men encountered them in 1540-41, they lived in scattered villages built around a ceremonial square, primarily within a stretch of land from the river to a perimeter extending about 25 miles outward. For them, the supreme deity was associated with the sky, sun, and fire.

The Chickasaws were not the first to choose the bluffs. The area's history rivals ancient Mediterranean

But the intrigue of multi-cultural mysteries, layers of raw frontiersmanship, strategic location, dedication to an ideal, and sheer endurance made a city of Memphis—not once, but twice.

cultures, with Indian artifacts dating back for centuries. The mysterious Mound Builders left an incredible legacy, although no recorded history except in mounds throughout the central area edging the mighty river. Memphis, although an ancient site, was infant in culture and in modern history. But the intrigue of multi-cultural mysteries, layers of raw frontiersmanship, strategic location, dedication to an ideal, and sheer endurance made a city of Memphis—not once, but twice.

When Andrew Jackson was elected president, he was personally acquainted with Indian affairs in the Western Territory from the Creek War and from living in the territory. His policy and an act of Congress caused provisions for the Indian tribes to be removed from east of the Mississippi River, relocated in western areas not yet dominated by white settlers.

After the Indian treaty, the Chickasaws were among the nations moved to Indian Territory, and the strategic site on the bluff became a boom town for land speculators.

Founded in 1819, Memphis was incorporated in 1826 and chartered as a city in 1840. The city was the heart of a fertile agricultural domain, and promised potential as the hub for trade both east and west. Only five years after incorporation, cotton wagons from neighboring counties began the trade that doubled in numbers of bales every decade until the Civil War. When the Memphis & Charleston Railroad connected the city to the Atlantic Ocean in 1857, Memphis became second to New Orleans as a cotton market.

The Episcopal Church arrived later in Tennessee than other Protestant denominations and Catholicism. French fur traders and Spanish explorers along the Mississippi River spread Catholic doctrine, establishing missions as they mapped the mid-continent. Early settlers pushing through the wilderness westward over the mountains from North Carolina formed congregations of Presbyterians, Methodists, and Baptists—often anti-ritualistic and personally opposed to the Church of England.

Early explorers from England included a chaplain among the ships' passengers, and extant records show that they held services on land as well. Virginia Dare was the first Episcopalian born and christened in the present United States. The Church of England was official in the original tidewater colonies, and George Calvert of Maryland, created the first Lord Baltimore by King James I, resigned his office as principal Secretary of State when he entered the Roman Catholic church in 1625.

The history of the colonies in the 17th century is filled with wars between denominations, as well as between settler and native. A Toleration Act passed in Maryland in 1649 granted religious freedom, but it was repealed five years later. The oppressed Puritans, striving to reform the established church, transported to the colonies their aim—for reform, not for separation of church and state. The idea that a state could be neutral about religion was believed by very few people in the 17th century. Not until the first amendment of our Constitution was a provision by law that government bodies could not dictate nor enforce religious affiliation.

In the Virginia colony, governed by the Crown, the Church of England was established by law in 1609 and a statute for compulsory church attendance was enacted but not enforced. In 1635, the Bishop of London was in charge of colonial churches, and was represented in the colonies by commissaries such as James Blair (1655-1743) in Virginia and Sir Thomas Bray (1656-1730) in Maryland. Early churchmen were missionaries, establishing schools and churches as they traveled among settlements. But the absence of a resident bishop and consequent lack of ordination in the colonies prevented growth.

One of the earliest Episcopal churches was Bruton Parish Church in Williamsburg, Virginia (after which St. John's was somewhat patterned), built in 1715. The parish was much older. Granite posts northwest of the church building mark the foundations of a small brick church built in 1683, and records show a parish rector in 1674. The adjacent cemetery is on land consecrated nearly a century before the 1715 building, and the oldest marker, dated 1678, seems to have been moved from another burial place. When the government of Virginia was moved from Jamestown to Williamsburg (1699) the influx of people to the parish outgrew the small early church, which had been built in Jacobean style. The present church has been in continual use since 1715.

Prominent in the history of Bruton Parish Church and commemorated by the largest old monument in the cemetery, the Bray family gave land for church use. Colonel David Bray was on the Vestry when the 1715 building was erected. Coincidentally, the name is repeated in the history of St. John's: the land for the original St. John's Chapel may have been given by Edmund Dozier Bray.

Episcopalians in the colonies tried repeatedly for an episcopate in their country. However, political and religious dissension over the issue delayed approval; the Bishop of London refused to ordain men for work in the new country.

The first bishop of the Church in America, Dr. Samuel Seabury, Jr., could not obtain approval in London, and was consecrated by non-juring bishops in Scotland in 1784. The Protestant Episcopal Church, independent of the Church

Bruton Parish,
Williamsburg, VA

of England, held an organizing convention in Philadelphia in 1789. By 1792 five bishops had been named.

The Revolutionary War fostered backlash against the Episcopal Church, and the estimated 500,000 communicants in 1775, depleted by Loyalist emigration, were not able to expand parishes westward as quickly as other Protestant denominations.

The earliest religious services recorded in Memphis were led by a slave called "Uncle Harry Lawrence," who preached in the home of William Lawrence.

One foggy Sunday morning in March 1822, from the deck of a flatboat on the Wolf River, Elijah Coffey "... had translated the contents of the Holy Scripture into his head, and when he opened his lips the Word was before the People." The Rev. Mr. Coffey had drifted down from Illinois to bring the gospel to the rowdy little settlement. He stayed, making his living as a shoemaker and preaching on the side. Another evangelist of the time was The Rev.

...planting the Episcopal faith in West Tennessee.

Mr. Silas Toncray—silversmith, watchmaker, engraver, sign painter, doctor, dentist, and druggist. When he died, he was eulogized in the daily newspaper as "a good man in the Christian sense of the term." These early preachers gave sermons to all who listened in Professor Eugene Magevney's log schoolhouse in Court Square.

Many of the services were held by circuit riders, who saddled up a horse, and, packing a Bible and a gun, treked through the wilderness that was West Tennessee.

The first Episcopal church in Tennessee was organized in Franklin, by The Rev. Mr. James Otey, in 1827.

The Diocese of Tennessee was formed in Nashville July 1, 1829. In 1832, The Rt. Rev. Levi Silliman Ives, second Bishop of North Carolina, organized the Tennessee Diocesan Convention. Among the attendees in Nashville were Thomas Wright and Samuel George Litton, who was ordained as Deacon on June 28, 1832.

The Rev. Mr. Thomas Wright and Mr. Litton came down the Mississippi on the *Tobacco Plant* steamboat and held services at Memphis—planting the Episcopal faith in West Tennessee.

In Memphis, the first Episcopal congregation of 10 members was organized in 1832 by The Rev. Mr. Wright. Services were held in the ecumenical building in Court Square. "Magevney's Academy" was the first meeting house, erected in 1826 with contributions from all classes. Population of the settlement at the beginning of the 1830s was 663; it was 1,700 by 1840.

The *Randolph Recorder* lists the death of The Rev. Mr. Thomas Wright only two years later, but he had succeeded in founding an Episcopal Church. Religious events were reported in the newspapers, although they didn't get the inches of space allocated to the daily theatre review.

American Quarterly Register gives the number of clergymen in the U.S. in 1834 as 14,000. Westward expansion created opportunities for preachers whose denominations had less stringent requirements for ordination. The Protestant Episcopal Church, however, followed more strict rules.

January 14, 1834, at St. Peter's Church in Philadelphia, James Hervey Otey was consecrated Bishop of Tennessee and appointed missionary bishop of the Southwest.

All of the country south of Kentucky and Missouri, from the eastern coast of Florida to the Pacific was his territory. In the thinly settled country, with no railroads and few public highways, he traveled among his people.

Calvary Parish was organized in 1832, as the establishment of churches moved across the state of Tennessee into the sparsely settled western region. Among the earliest settlers, when the western district was opened about the time of the Treaty with the Chickasaws, were the Anderson B. and Thomas D. Carr families. Among the incorporating communicants of Calvary was the wife of a planter who gave land in 1866 to the Diocese of Tennessee for what may have been the first building for St. John's.

Eliza Brothers Bray was one of the 10 original members of Calvary. In 1838, her husband, Edmund Dozier Bray, owned and farmed 200 acres of Island No. 46 in the Mississippi River. The young couple gave their address in the 1840 census as "Shelby County." Edmund, born in 1811, was not listed as one of the charter members of Calvary, but was No. 21 in the list of the first 21 members in 1839-40 compiled by the third Rector, The Rev. Mr. Philip Alston (Eliza was No. 9). Edmund was a lay delegate from Calvary to the Convention at Randolph in 1839.

The Great Book of Calvary says that "Several of the families of the Church lived in Memphis' plantation environs and with problems of distance and transportation, their attendance regularly at services was uncertain. Among these were the families of Samuel Rembert, Colonel John Pope, Edmund Bray, Thomas Beatty, and probably the Cary-Skipwith family."

Like many churches, Calvary sold or rented pews annually to support the church and Rector. Both St. Mary's and Grace Church advertised free pews. From the pew charts it is possible to learn some of the communicants who attended Calvary. Edmund Bray was listed in the 1846 Pew Chart as having Pew No. 17, on the right aisle near the back. He also was listed that year as a subscriber to the Diocese Missionary Society.

Many of the early settlers, including Edmund and Eliza Bray, came from North Carolina. Many of those who pioneered in Episcopal churches in West Tennessee came from Calvary Protestant Episcopal Church in Wadesboro, North Carolina. Bishop Otey, however, was born in Virginia. He was baptized and confirmed on the same day at

The Episcopal Church as a whole was not yet on firm ground in the mid-19th century.

St. John's Episcopal Church in Williamsboro, North Carolina, when he was 24 and ordained as Deacon the following year in the same church.

The Episcopal Church as a whole was not yet on firm ground in the mid-19th century. In 1854, in Washington, D.C., a young woman begging alms door-to-door fell dead. Her husband died in the alms house a few days later. Their 5-year-old orphan daughter was claimed by an aunt in England who wrote to the Washington Orphan Asylum to get the child. The city was shocked to learn that the poor dead couple were highly connected. He was an Episcopal minister of the Church of England. Her sister was married to a colonel in the British army. They had starved to death.

In Memphis, Calvary Episcopal Church prospered, building the first Episcopal church and organizing two missions: Grace Church in 1850 and St. Mary's in 1853. They were admitted to the Diocese at the Convention in 1858.

For two decades, Calvary was the only Episcopal church in Memphis. The beautiful new building had a ceiling problem, and the congregation met in other locations while it was repaired. On January 16, 1847, the *Daily Enquirer* announced "Services of the Episcopal Church tomorrow at Hightower's Hall, on Shelby Street between Union Street and the Gayoso House, at the usual hour." Services in February were held in the office of H. G. Smith, Esq., on Jefferson Street, with The Rev. Mr. P. W. Alston officiating.

Bishop Otey moved from Columbia, Tennessee to Memphis in 1852, and probably helped to organize a "Ladies Educational and Missionary Society" in 1853. He

The railway connection helped to create a boom in land sales for areas outside the city limits—such as around Buntyn's Station—and helped to make a community of the planters in the area. It was the soil in which St. John's was planted.

preached at Calvary in 1855-56 when there was no rector, and served as rector there in 1858-59 "only until a permanent could be found." His other duties, ministering to many parishes, evidently took too much time. In October 1859—while Bishop Otey was out of town—the Vestry called The Rev. Dr. George White. The election was on a

Monday night; he returned on Thursday morning. Bishop Otey wrote a letter stating that they knew he would be home in a few days, and the "Vestry could have lost nothing by awaiting my return . . . especially since my term of service had not expired by nearly 3 months."

The city also prospered, with cotton from the fertile farmland increasing profits and population. Early businesses in Memphis between 1840 and 1877 included *The Appeal*, Orgill Brothers, John A. Denie's Sons Co., Oak Hall, Seessel's, and Burke's Book Store. By 1843, there were three banks in Memphis. The Memphis and Charleston Railroad, chartered in Tennessee in 1846, finally opened in 1857. The Pigeon Roost and Chulahoma Turnpike Company, chartered February 1, 1850, was capitalized at $41,000. David Greer was one of the directors for establishing the plank toll-road.

The Memphis & Charleston Railroad ran the first train as far as Col. Eppy White's farm on Saturday, July 24, 1852. There was a big barbeque to celebrate. By September 21, trains began to run regularly to Germantown. The railway connection helped to create a boom in land sales for areas outside the city limits—such as around Buntyn's Station—and helped to make a community of the planters in the area. It was the soil in which St. John's was planted.

In 1978, St. John's celebrated 100 years of history, securely verified with records of its illustrious, rollercoaster past. But *The Commercial Appeal's* nod to the past threw in a new date. An item in "Bygone Days" suggested that the church was older.

Microfilm reels later, it evolved that the date for the

little mention was off by a few days. And Memphis had six major newspapers in the latter part of the 19th century. Buntyn was then called "Oaklawn," and references were obscure. But finally some of the facts emerged in print.

By the mid-1850s, the plank road ran past Mr. Bray's. By 1854 the Pigeon Roost Plank Road was completed 25 miles out. The Memphis charity hospital was incorporated on Pigeon Roost Road, 1 1/4 miles from the then city limits.

In 1854, Edmund Bray and Geraldus Buntyn were among the attorneys delegated by the court as commissioners to appraise, evaluate, and divide up slaves to the Eckles heirs.

General Geraldus Buntyn, from whom the area took its name, came to Memphis following the War of 1812. He received a land grant of 160 acres for his services in the war. He owned property in the City of Memphis, but especially was among the land speculators of Shelby County in the late 1840s and 1850s. In 1856 he wrote a will bequeathing more than 1,400 acres of land in Shelby County to his heirs.

Another successful land speculator of the time was David Greer, whose Indian trading post in Paris, Tennessee, became a retail business when population of the area changed to white settlers. Mr. Greer then started a bank in Holly Springs, Mississippi, but it failed in the financial panic of 1837. He came to Shelby County, and bought up land in the rapidly appreciating southeastern area near Buntyn's Station.

Most prominent in the history of St. John's is another early settler from North Carolina who came to then Oaklawn in 1843—Judge John Lewis Taylor Sneed. He was a devout Episcopalian.

Shrouded in the mists of suburban obscurity, the origins of St. John's still elude substantiation. That the church is older than its perceived inception of 1878 is clear; how much older is still a mystery.

When the Peabody Hotel was built in the mid-19th century, Memphis already seemed the beginning of the Delta—as a familiar quote later popularized. Second only to New Orleans as a spot cotton market, Memphis was the sixth largest city in the South at the beginning of the Civil War. The city was predicted to be the "New York of the South," surpassing both St. Louis and

The city was predicted to be the "New York of the South..."

New Orleans as mid-continent trade center, until the second half of the 19th century nearly wrote Memphis to history, with war, epidemic plagues, and financial reversal.

Key to both expansion and exposure for the area was the access by both turnpike and railroad.

Prosperous planters in LaGrange chartered the Memphis & LaGrange Railroad in 1835, to be 49 miles of access to get cotton shipments to the Mississippi River. The railroad started at Memphis but only got as far as Buntyn—about six miles out—when the financial crisis of 1837-38 killed the project. The right of way had been laid as far as White's Station—nine miles out—and the valuable access was acquired by the Memphis & Charleston when it was chartered.

The Memphis & Charleston Railroad, chartered in 1846, opened nearly 11 years later after difficulties and dissension about the long delays. In 1850 the Pigeon Roost and Chulahoma (sic) Turnpike Company was chartered, to build a plank road route along what is now Lamar. The County Court ruled " . . . that Edward Elam oversee the Pigeon Roost Road from Nonconnah Bridge to Z. Alvis' old place with the hands that worked under the former overseer." Pigeon Roost Road and Stateline Road (Poplar) formed a wedge fanning out to White's Station, with the Memphis & Charleston Railroad bisecting horizontally.

Completion of the railroad was honored with festivities in both cities. A barrel of water from the Mississippi River was carried on a flat car attached to the special train to Charleston. There, a fire engine pumped the water into the Atlantic Ocean. The process was reversed, with water from the Atlantic brought to the Mississippi, acclaimed as a "Marriage of the Waters." Early in the war control of the railroad became priority; part of the railroad was controlled by each side.

Early in the war control of the railroad became priority...

As war became imminent, newspaper articles advocated for both sides of the conflict. Divergence of opinion reflected the bifurcation of the crisis. The river and the railroad put the city in a strategic position. The daily newspaper with the Confederate viewpoint began urging armament with heavy guns, in early spring before the short battle for control of the city. The editorial page quoted a letter that the Hon. John L.T. Sneed had written to a friend in Washington that "a collision between the Federal troops and the soldiers of the South would, in a very few days, convert the state of Tennessee into a vast military camp." The editorial concluded that "The collision has occurred."

With the start of the Civil War, mobility became difficult. Completion of railroad linkage to other cities, however, and accelerated road projects to complete plank roads in Shelby County worked both for and against the area. It gave access to outlying areas, faster trips between the County Court in Raleigh Springs and Main Street, and increased property values outside the city limits. It fostered growth of suburban areas such as Oaklawn (south of the railroad) and Buntyn (across the track). The railroad was necessary in moving troops and supplies to the war-torn interior.

The Navy Yard at Memphis was ceded by Congress to the City in 1854, after long debates by the city whether to accept. It became strategic in the war effort, and was reclaimed as government property.

Union forces occupied Memphis early in the Civil War, and many of the mercantile aristocracy left. But its strategic location made the city a center for contraband trade. The population doubled within a decade.

Fearing the approach of the Federal troops, farmers in Shelby County began to burn their cotton on May 31, 1861, creating economic hardship for the agrarian community.

The fierce battle on the river was short. Federal gunboats breached security to attack Island No. 10 and moved into the harbor at Memphis.

Memphis fell on June 6, 1862, and many of the churches were seized to be used as hospitals, barracks, or stables for the Union troops. Houses, trees, fences, and churches were torn down. General Sherman wrote that "Armies in motion or stationary must commit some waste . . . (that) is the natural consequence of war . . . Generally, war is destruction and nothing else."

Sherman's arrival to take command in Memphis was announced in *The Daily Bulletin* newspaper (the Federal viewpoint) on Sunday, July 20, saying that, following "his brilliant conduct at Shiloh," Sherman had been on the road from Corinth to Memphis since the evacuation of Corinth.

"... Generally, war is destruction and nothing else."
– General Sherman

In July, an advertisement in the newspaper "by order of Gen. U. S. Grant" decreed that all Confederate sympathizers must leave the city within less than a week. "All holding office, or employed by the so-called Confederacy" were suddenly refugees, moving to outlying areas wherever they had relatives. The published order stated that they must declare whether "they are loyal, or disloyal, or aliens. If they claim to be loyal, they must take the oath of allegiance. Those who fail to do so will be held as enemies. Those who declare themselves enemies cannot vote, cannot go to law, hold any place or carry on any business, and they will be sent beyond the lines." Articles published soon after noted that giving aid and comfort "to the public enemy" was punishable by death. Citizens of Memphis were urged to register. "An entire year of occupation in this city" had given ample opportunity to register . . . "to make their deliberate election of the sovereignty to which they owe their allegiance." Article X of the publication (May 27, 1863) announced that "All real estate of registered enemies will be liable for seizure by the United States."

Since Memphis was "an insurrectionary city," cotton was taken by the Federals to be sold in a non-rebel state. In June, 800 bales of "Government cotton" were lying in Memphis, waiting for a determination whether it would be shipped to St. Louis or to Cincinnati for sale. The last sale held in Memphis was 1,160 bales, sold at an average of 35 1/2 cents per pound. Termination of the cotton trade was a death decree to Shelby County's main source of profit and employment.

Local news in June stated that about 100 refugees— mostly women and children— from Glendale, on the Memphis & Charleston Railroad, were at the wharf to leave the city, since they had lost their homes "as a consequence of following Jefferson Davis' rebellion." Residents loyal to either side found themselves at odds with neighbors, relatives, and religion, since many residents of the young city were immigrants who held convictions confirmed in other regions.

The struggle of loyalty between church and state continued throughout the war. Many of the city's ministers had relocated from areas now on the opposite side in the conflict from their parishioners. Sermons urged prayer for the nation as well as for the troops.

Many ministers in the city were not sympathetic to secession, and strife in the church ensued. Some denominations, such as Methodists and Baptists, had split into northern and southern segments as much as 15 years before. The Episcopal Church nationally remained united. Bishop Otey, although a Southerner to heart, dearly loved the idea of one nation, and struggled with the need to accommodate either South or North in his services.

At Calvary, Dr. George White sympathized with the Union and many of the Federal officers attended services at Calvary. To Confederates, it was the ultimate outrage. The Rector was torn between the mindset of his parish and what he deemed true to his office. An outraged parishioner wrote a letter to the *Appeal* protesting against the prayers for the Union, and clergymen decided to use only the communion service, which contained no prayers

Sermons urged prayer for the nation as well as for the troops.

for secular rulers. A group with strong Confederate ties broke away from Calvary and formed St. Lazarus Church—named, it was said, not for the saint, but . . . "representing Lazarus whose sores were licked by dogs." At the end of July 1861, Bishop Otey issued a pastoral letter announcing the secession of the Diocese of Tennessee from The General Convention of the Protestant Episcopal Church. With Tennessee's secession from the Union, the diocese could no longer be a member of the Episcopal Church in the United States of America. The General Convention in 1862 urged southern delegates, conspicuous by their absence, to practice brotherly love. The South was not fully represented again until 1868.

Dr. White's efforts to ameliorate conflict in the church alienated him from both sides. *The Daily Bulletin* often reported with suspicion about churches, and Calvary was under scrutiny. When President Lincoln decreed a day of thanksgiving for the success in quelling rebellion, the newspaper reported that not one Episcopal church was open on that Thursday, August 6, 1863. Further, it stated that The Rev. Dr. White, Rector of Calvary, had gone to Canada for the duration of the war. The story proved incorrect when Dr. White was in the pulpit as usual by early September. Meantime, services were held the following Sunday by The Rev. Mr. Wheelock, with attendance about average, although the prayer for the President was omitted.

Churches were strong influences upon daily life in the mid-19th century. Ministers were especially suspect by both sides, if the tone of newspaper articles reflect accurately. References to difficulties were often noted in the *Bulletin* in relation to religion, such as a news item that cotton was burned "near the place of Rev. Mr. J. W. Knoft."

...although the prayer for the President was omitted.

In September that year, the newspaper sent a reporter on "a little circuit last Sabbath among city churches." He reported that most were open. The Rev. Dr. White was in the pulpit at Calvary, although, according to the reporter, he "mutilated the beautiful service" by leaving out any reference to secular leaders. The report listed each church within the city, and whether services were held, noting that St. Mary's was not open, but that it was ascertained that the Rector, Mr. Hines, held the morning service at Grace Church and would open St. Mary's for 3:00 p.m. service.

Only two weeks later a scene occurred at Calvary, when the service was interrupted by Gen. Thomas, Adjutant General of the United States, loudly repeating the entire passage that The Rev. Dr. White omitted from the service. Long letters on the editorial page reviled churches for the abridged service and the dissension it created.

Whether because many of the communicants of Episcopal churches were planters, lawyers, and bankers who represented the financial sector, or because many officers of the occupying forces were Episcopalian, or because the church wielded power, newspapers highlighted church-related activities. Perhaps, it was because such activities were time-honored coalitions of power, establishing community from diversity. Whatever the rationale, the Episcopal Church in West Tennessee suffered—not only churches within Memphis, but throughout the region.

St. Louis protested a proposition to reestablish the Navy Yard at Memphis, declaring that it would make the city a worthy target for the rebels to reclaim. But the Mississippi River was considered key to guarding the city. On June 18, 1863, General Order No. 70 of the Headquarters District of Memphis outlined the boundaries as Wolf River on the north, Nonconnah Creek on the south, a line drawn from the Wolf south through White's Station to Nonconnah as the eastern boundary, and the Mississippi on the west.

The Memphis & Charleston Railroad was the strategic artery into the city. After the occupation of Memphis by Federal forces, many of the minor skirmishes in the area were provoked by subversive attacks on the railroad by Confederate guerrilla forces. Although by July 3 over 10,000 people in Memphis had taken the oath of loyalty, outlying areas remained rebel. LaGrange suffered higher suspicion, but skirmishes along Nonconnah Creek and the Buntyn area brought retribution to the perpetrators.

In October 1863 a rebel force reported to be 5,000-8,000 strong tried to break the link between Memphis and

The financial vicissitudes of war affected Memphis for the remainder of the decade.

Corinth by repeated attacks on the Memphis & Charleston Railroad. Fearful of continuing attacks, paymasters went under heavy guard when they took the Memphis & Charleston out to pay the troops. Men who previously were regarded as good citizens had become raiders; some for the cause in which they believed, some for survival. But whatever the cause, it made any travel hazardous, and travel on the M&C between Memphis and LaGrange particularly dangerous.

As troops advanced, attacked, reconnoitered, and died in the triangle of Memphis, LaGrange, and Corinth, river and railroad access dominated strategy.

The financial vicissitudes of war affected Memphis for the remainder of the decade. An open letter in *The Public Ledger*, March 17, 1869, asks "all area members and friends of the Protestant Episcopal Church" in and near Memphis to help pay off the debt on the residence of the late Bishop Otey. The house on Poplar was bought for $12,000 by the Diocese in January 1866, with $7,000 paid in cash and the balance mortgaged. The property was to be held as a residence for the "Bishop of the Diocese to which Memphis should belong." The letter says that "the great distress in money matters" prevented paying the debt, and that the house was to be resold for debts, losing both the residence for a Bishop and the initial investment by the Diocese. The signers petitioned that all friends help to raise the money. Further, that Bishop Quintard had paid $1,000 of the original amount and would contribute $2,000 more if the additional $5,000 could be raised by interested Episcopalians in the Memphis area. If sufficient money was not raised, any money contributed would be refunded. One of the signers of the letter was John Cubbins, who gave five acres at Pine Street and Carnes (two blocks from the old St. John's church) to the Diocese in 1869, for the sum of $5 (probably a transfer fee).

Bitter debates nationally over the valuation of currency led to Black Friday—September 24, 1869—when the price of gold plunged from 162 to 135, ruining many speculators. Public debt grew and states raised tax burdens, especially in the former Confederate states, while property values plummeted.

3

The history of St. John's Episcopal Church reflects the mid-19th century turbulence of wars, plagues, and social upheaval in Memphis. Birthed in the Civil War—probably in social and economic forces leading up to the war—St. John's faithful congregation shaped policy of the region as well as the parish. Lists of parishioners read like pages from a "Who's Who in Memphis History." Events converged to form the infant parish.

It's easy to substantiate the history from the late 1870s, but, in fact, the parish was well established before that time. It was probably born during the early 1850s. A

St. John's faithful congregation shaped policy of the region as well as the parish.

tantalizing article in a newspaper of just after the war gives the beginning as 1854, and relates that the church was burned during a raid by Union forces (1864?). There are three primary reasons it is so hard to substantiate: 1) that property for a church would have been held in trust by some parishioner, since there was no incorporated entity for ownership; 2) that Diocesan records are not comprehensive for the middle part of the 19th century, being interrupted by war; and, 3) that the parish records burned when the firebug struck the Loaring-Clark library in 1937, destroying all the old church documents.

Also, Buntyn, outside the city limits by a few miles, was different from Memphis. Records for the City are more complete than records for Shelby County, since the numerous newspapers did not always include outlying areas in the columns on local news.

The suburb of Buntyn grew up around the Buntyn's Station stop on the Memphis and Charleston Railroad. Bought by the Southern Railroad in 1898, the tracks parallel Southern Avenue in the Buntyn neighborhood. In the mid-19th century, Buntyn was established about six miles east and slightly south of Memphis. The area was named for Geraldus Buntyn, a soldier in the War of 1812, who came from North Carolina temporarily through Alabama to Memphis, and began buying land in Shelby County in the 1830s. In 1842 he gave a lot with a small frame house (about where the Court House is now) for the First Baptist Church. His elaborate home in Buntyn later became

The suburb of Buntyn grew up around the Buntyn's Station stop on the Memphis and Charleston Railroad.

the first home of the Memphis Country Club (bought in 1905, burned in 1910). He defined the area in which St. John's grew, but he was not a participant in the growth. Instead, he was a founder of First Baptist Church and later supported the Baptist church at Poplar and Perkins.

Judge John Lewis Taylor Sneed, a devout Episcopalian, moved from North Carolina to Buntyn in 1843 (then called Oaklawn). Judge Sneed served in the Mexican War, moved to Hardeman County, then to Bolivar, then to Shelby County. In antebellum days he was elected Attorney General of Tennessee.

Born in 1811, he survived the Mexican War, the Civil War (as a brigadier general—fighting between the sessions of the Confederate legislature, of which he was a member), yellow fever, taxation, and political intrigue. When he died, just as the century changed, he was eulogized by

No one was fired with a more romantic zeal at that time than John L. T. Sneed . . .

newspapers as one of the "romantic young fellows [who] stepped out of Scott's novels, clad in their unique Highland costume, to make war against the successors of the Montezumas. No one was fired with a more romantic zeal at that time than John L. T. Sneed, though there never was any malice in his heart toward a single human being."

After the war he returned to practicing law, served on the Tennessee Supreme Court, as chancellor of Shelby County, as President of Memphis Law School (1887-1893), and as Chancellor of the Chancery Court. He was called one of the ablest jurists of the South.

And he was "an ardent Shakespearean student, and when he found one who was kindred with himself in love for the great poet he could talk by the hour, pouring out in exquisite word and flowing phrase his devotion and admiration."

Edmund Dozier and Eliza Bray, among the first members of Calvary Church, also owned land near Buntyn. Edmund Dozier Bray was a good friend of Bishop Otey. Edward Elam was Edmund Bray's neighbor, and they jointly gave land for a chapel.

St. John's was birthed out of such seemingly unrelated facts, although the date of the actual event has not been substantiated.

The few extant records suggest that there was a group of worshippers before the chapel was built. Whether the mission was called "Otey Chapel" before Bishop Otey's death (1863) is unclear.

Probably the first building for St. John's was the chapel attached to the Church Home. Where the mission was established and where the small group met is unknown. Since the orphanage was established by women, it may have been difficult to document a congregation attached to it. According to the *Journal of the Proceedings of the Twenty-Eighth Annual Convention of the Clergy and Laity of the Protestant Episcopal Church in the Diocese of Tennessee* (1856), if the communicants were female, (they) "of course (could) make no direct efforts towards the organization of a congregation, although earnestly desirous of enjoying the privileges of the Church."

But, according to the same report, "Church Families are becoming estranged from the Church because there is no room for them in the Church." The number of pews at Calvary was 72, to seat 140 families. Pew rents were high, due to the increased demand. The report continued that "Thus, . . . not only the poor, but even persons of moderate means will be excluded from the Church, and compelled to seek a spiritual home elsewhere." This growth period evidently fostered new missions, such as Grace

Church and Church of the Good Shepherd. However, Grace Church evidently lost momentum a few years after it was organized in 1850, reorganized in 1856, and was not admitted to the Diocese until 1858.

Throughout the 19th century the struggle for existence left many children homeless. Bishop Otey preached a sermon at Calvary in February 1859 about the need for charity in behalf of the Orphan's Asylum.

In January 1869, *The Daily Memphis Avalanche* stated that "A post office has been established at Buntyn's Station, on the Memphis & Charleston Railroad, and the name adopted is 'OakLawn,' J. H. McClure, Postmaster."

A History of Saint John's Parish, written in 1938 by Elizabeth Saunders Ramsay, relates that:

"The Church Home was originally located in Buntyn on the southwest corner of Semmes and Spottswood and about four and a half miles southwest was the location of the Otey Chapel on the old Tchulahoma Road."

"There will be divine worship at the Episcopal Church Home, at Buntyn Station, this afternoon."

The first recorded burial in the cemetery attached to Otey Chapel was in 1844—the five-year-old daughter of Mr. and Mrs. J. W. Elam. Another daughter, not quite seven, was buried there in 1844; their 15-year-old son joined them in 1851. Eliza Brothers Bray was buried there in 1866.

That year (1866) Edmund Dozier Bray gave 10 acres to the Diocese for a church, and, with the help of his neighbor J. W. Elam, evidently built the first chapel. On Sunday, August 15, 1869, a religious notice in *The Daily Memphis Avalanche* stated that:

"There will be divine worship at the Episcopal Church Home, at Buntyn Station, this afternoon. A special train leaves the Memphis & Charleston depot at half-past four o'clock and returns at half-past six. Fare for the round trip is twenty-five cents. The lady managers of the Home will be glad to see the services numerously attended, and expect them to be held every Sunday afternoon."

The Bishop's Address in the Diocesan Journal for 1866 states that he "rode out ten miles to Otey Chapel" on Saturday, April 14. "After morning prayer by the Rev.

"He has done what he could, and the Lord will bless him."

J. M. Schwrar, priest-in-charge, I preached, baptized an adult and confirmed eleven candidates, and delivered an address. Mr. Schwrar is doing most faithful work, and will no doubt succeed in establishing a strong parish at this place. Mr. Bray, a faithful layman of the church, who first started the work of the church in this neighborhood, and who built the chapel, has conveyed to the Convention of the Protestant Episcopal Church of Tennessee, the church building and ten acres of ground. He has done what he could, and the Lord will bless him."

The Journal from the convention in 1867 states that The Rev. Mr. J. M. Schwrar "accepted a call to (Immanuel Church, LaGrange) in June last, to officiate two Sundays in each month, thus leaving two Sundays for Otey Chapel, Shelby County." In his report for Otey Chapel, he stated that "My support since January 1st has been derived from the offerings for that purpose on the second Sunday of each month; before that time, chiefly from E. D. Bray, whose hearty zeal for the Church is worthy of imitation."

The Bishop's address to the Convention in 1869 praised a sermon at Calvary by The Rev. Mr. E. A. Bradley, who "has for many years occupied a high position in the commercial world, and has now given himself to the work of Christ. . . . Since his ordination, he has been doing service as Chaplain to the Church Home, Memphis, and assisting the clergy in the several parishes of the city."

His journal notes on Tuesday, April 20th: "I laid the foundation stone of the Orphanage of the Church Charity Foundation. Addresses were delivered by the Rev. Dr. White and myself. This house is to be erected on ground generously donated by Mrs. Speed and her sister, Mrs. Spottswood. Three hundred and fifty-five dollars were contributed at the laying of the corner-stone."

The connection between the Church Home and Otey Chapel—beyond geographical proximity—is unclear from old records. They evidently were not associated as in more recent history. The Rev. Mr. Schwrar reported to the 1869 Convention that: "Since last September I have officiated at the Church Home, at Buntyn's Station, on the second Sunday afternoon of each month, and on an occasional fifth Sunday morning . . . and have given the Home as much pastoral attention as other engagements would permit. Having resigned the parish of LaGrange, I intend, the Lord willing, to devote the second and fourth Sundays of the month to the Church Home, and the first and third to Otey Chapel."

The Rev. Mr. Richard Hines preached in the chapel of the Church Home on August 8, 1869. The newspaper account states that the Church Home was at Oak Lawn, on the Memphis & Charleston Railroad. Another article just two days previously states that:

"It is said Buntyn's Station, on the Memphis & Charleston Railroad, is going ahead rapidly. A number of building lots have been sold there of late. It is only five miles out and promises to become an important place of residence for people doing business in the City."

From 1850 to the late 1860s, newspaper articles mentioned various groups who attempted to establish homes for the many orphans. The Episcopal Church Home—called the "Church Charity Foundation of the Protestant Episcopal Church in the City of Memphis"—was among those established that survived. Others are Porter-Leath and St. Peter's.

The Church Home was originally downtown, and was partially funded by ice cream socials organized by some concerned women. The Home moved from Market Street to Shelby Street, to Buntyn's Station, and, after only a short period, moved back into the city.

The new orphanage in Buntyn was built on 10 acres of land given by Mrs. John H. Speed and Mrs. E. A. Spottswood. It was dedicated in 1869. The chapel was called "St. John's." In 1870, the name for the orphanage became the "Church Orphans' Home" and the managers were called the "Lady Associates of the Church Home."

By 1871 the little church had achieved parish status, with 31 communicants. That year, Edmund Dozier Bray was a lay delegate from St. John's to the annual Convention. Since services were held on alternate weeks at Otey Chapel and at the Church Home, it may be that parishioners worshipped at both places.

The Rev. Mr. Peter Wager recorded in his diary that

Bishop Otey Memorial Chapel at Tchulahoma and Raines

he was appointed chaplain of the Church Home and missionary to St. John's and Otey Chapel in the fall of 1871. He preached at St. John's for the first time in late October. When the Church Home moved to Jackson Avenue on February 12, 1873, the Reverend Mr. Wager moved to Memphis and resigned as missionary for St. John's after increasing the size of the congregation considerably.

Services continued for some time, but, according to Mrs. Ramsay's history of St. John's, the property was sold to the Cliosophic Society on September 1, 1877. The Society permitted the congregation to continue holding services there, whenever a preacher was available.

Otey Chapel and St. John's had a different tie a century later, when Otey Chapel became a mission of St. John's. There was then no building for Otey Chapel at the old location of Tchulahoma Road, but the land was again made available. Many of the architectural elements from the old Otey Chapel and from the summer retreat for the children, St. Mary's in the Woods, at Hardy, Arkansas, were combined in the new building, including an old "Tiffany" window (luminous stained glass designed in the 19th century by Louis Comfort Tiffany) and a Tiffany-style window. In 1961, St. John's agreed to sponsor the Chapel for five years, at which time the feasibility would be reassessed.

The Rev. Mr. John P. Davis, Jr., became Vicar in July 1962, and, for a few years, the parish prospered. However, changing neighborhood demographics and rumors of possible airport annexation and buyout of the area created difficulties in maintaining a strong parish. Mr. Davis reported to St. John's Vestry in January 1968 that he felt the chaplain's work of the Church Home could be handled without the need of a Vicar, and that anyone serving as rector of Otey Chapel might be utilized as a part-time assistant at St. John's instead.

A Tiffany stained glass window over the altar of Bishop Otey Memorial Chapel

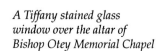

Mr. Davis resigned in 1968; The Rev. Mr. Richard Maddock was called by Otey as the new Vicar. The Church Home Board continued some support to Otey Chapel through 1970. Under Mr. Maddock's leadership, the Parish Building was renovated in 1970 and all buildings repainted.

There was substantial growth in the Oak Haven area in 1971, which led to discussion of the possibility that Otey Chapel might become a full Parish or a Diocesan Mission.

In 1974, Mr. Maddock resigned. It was concluded by members of Otey Chapel, St. John's, and Bishop Gates that "there was not a viable congregation at Otey." The Vestry of St. John's negotiated with Youth Service for use of the property. Otey Chapel was deeded back to the Diocese on June 17, 1974.

The story of the land continued. The family of the original grantors again gave the ten acres at Raines and Tchulahoma to the Diocese of Tennessee in 1985, with the agreement that the small cemetery be maintained.

The mission of the Church Home changed from being an orphanage to instead meet other needs of children. The program has served children who need shelter because of family difficulties. It changed again in the mid-1970s to be a residential training center for autistic children.

Whether or not the chapel of the Church Home was the first building called "St. John's," it was a name very dear to Bishop Otey:

Baptised & confirmed   1824 St. John's, Williamsboro, NC
Lay Delegate to Eighth
    Annual Convention 1824   "   "   "   "

Ordained Deacon   1825   "   "   "   "
Consecrated church   1847 St. John's, Bedford, VA (near his birthplace), in September 1847, acting in behalf of the Bishop of Virginia and at the request of the Wardens and Vestry of Heber Parish.
Buried   1865 St. John's Ashwood, near Columbia, TN

*He died in 1863, during the Civil War, and his body was temporarily put into the Leatherman vault at Elmwood, then buried when the war ended.

Edmund Dozier Bray died in 1880 and is buried in the Otey Chapel Cemetery.

Yellow Fever

4

Hughetta Snowden rode out to Buntyn with Bishop Charles Todd Quintard in 1870 to see the new Church Home. Despite poverty, the home was utterly clean and orderly. Hughetta went to see a cell of one of the Sisters, and later described it in her memoirs as white-washed walls, spotlessly scrubbed floors, with a white cotton curtain at the window, a small room furnished with a plain deal chair, narrow cot with a snowy coverlet, and small pillow. A small table held a Bible, manuals of devotion, a Crucifix, and two candlesticks. A small vase with a few fragrant roses stood before the Crucifix. When the Sister died in 1871 the orphanage moved from Buntyn, relocating near St. Mary's Church.

In November 1872, consent was given for St. Mary's Convent in New York (founded 1865) to establish an Episcopal school in Memphis. Although there had been a school named "St. Mary's," run as a parochial school of Calvary, it was not a convent school.

At a meeting of the Chapter the following May, it was decided to send four sisters to establish a chapter in Memphis, and they came in August 1873: Sister Hughetta and three others. Sister Constance (age 28) and the Novice (age 25) were sent ahead, allowing six weeks to prepare for opening a school. The Bishop's house was not yet in order, so the Mother arranged for them to stay just outside the city at Annesdale, with Sister Hughetta's brother and sister-in-law, Col. and Mrs. Robert Bogardus Snowden.

Sister Hughetta was born in Nashville in 1848, the daughter of John Bayard and Aspasia Seraphina Imogene Bogardus Snowden. She became Sister Superior of the Southern Work of St. Mary's in 1878. Sister Superior came to Memphis just as a tiny mosquito nearly destroyed the city.

The economic depression that started in 1873 lasted 66 months, but its devastation was minor compared to

Sister Superior came to Memphis just as a tiny mosquito nearly destroyed the city.

what the mosquito brought. Memphis' population was approximately 60,000 in 1873. Eight thousand people died in the epidemics of 1873, 1878, and 1879, decimating the earlier population by more than a tenth.

Through the early years of the century, newspaper accounts told of yellow fever in other cities. In Memphis, there had been two deaths from yellow fever in August 1855, more in October. Then the epidemic in 1873 hit.

Yellow fever broke out just as school was about to open in the fall of 1873. A newspaper account on September 15 says there were 25 deaths per day. The Sisters of

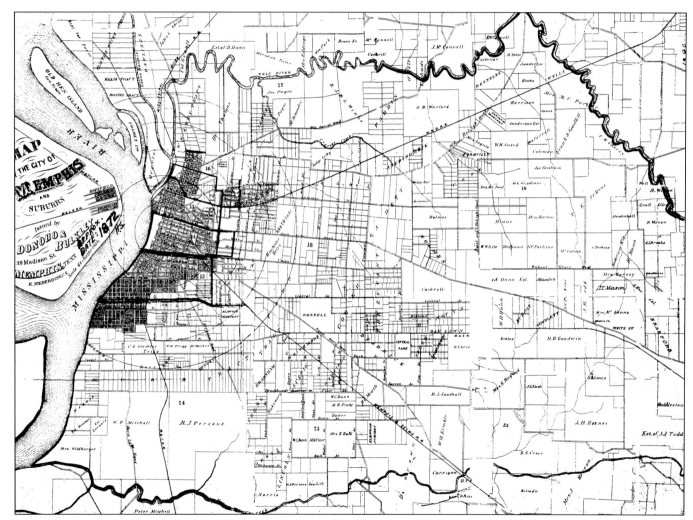

Map of the City of Memphis, ca. 1872

St. Mary's packed little baskets with things to help the sick and ministered to the victims, under direction of Dr. George Carroll Harris, Dean of St. Mary's Church, and a doctor who instructed the sisters. Sister Amelia was sent from Nashville to help. Sister Hughetta reported in her journal that they were frightened at first, but didn't get the fever.

When the epidemic was declared, Sister Amelia went to Buntyn to take charge of the Children's Home.

The school opened in October, when the fever abated, with 20 girls, eight of them residents. The epidemic was finally over in November, after a frost. At the new school, the Sisters taught mathematics, English composition, history, French, and Latin. They gave piano lessons. They visited the sick and the poor.

That year was only a forerunner of the terrible year of 1878, when 5,000 people died in 11 weeks between mid-

People fled from Memphis in panic, some helping to establish towns in a hub around the city, but never to return.

August and mid-November. Only one of the Sisters of St. Mary's escaped. Two Episcopal priests were among the victims: The Rev. Mr. Charles Carroll Parsons, Rector of St. Lazarus, and The Rev. Mr. Louis S. Schuyler, who died just two days after he came down from St. Louis to aid the sick.

People fled from Memphis in panic, some helping to establish towns in a hub around the city, but never to return. Since Buntyn was outside the city, the community seemed remote from the epidemic. Journals and newspaper articles describe the cautions to contain the epidemic from outlying areas.

Many of the residents left Buntyn, praying for an early frost. Although they had no knowledge of the dreadful disease's source, they knew it subsided with frost.

It was October, late in mosquito season, although not late enough for frost, that ghoulish plague struck Buntyn. The railroad that had brought development also brought devastation. Refugees who may not even have known they were ill when they began their escape from Memphis brought the disease to Buntyn when the railroad car in which they were riding was sidetracked at Buntyn's Station.

Addison Hayes and his wife, Peggy, could not leave the area because he had to keep the bank open. They rented Gen. Buntyn's former home in the country, hoping to evade the epidemic. With them came Peggy Hayes' brother, the young Jefferson Davis, Jr., the last living son of the Confederate leader. Each evening on the way home to the country, Addison Hayes fumigated himself before his return to his family in Buntyn. But Jefferson Davis caught the fever from a child, and died on October 16th, just as the fever waned.

It was the decade that delayed the progress of St. John's–probably due to both the economic and the health issues.

For more than two months in 1878 there were no public gatherings. Memphis was quarantined. Despite the appalling lack of sanitation, efforts were made to combat the deadly fever. Lime was spread and streets were soaked with carbolic acid.

Ironically, the epidemic gave St. John's the Semmes and Spottswood property.

The Cliosophic Literary Society was duly chartered in 1877 and, with James J. Richardson as President, signed a mortgage to buy property, which they had already designated as "Cliosophic Hall," to be used as a theatre. The property was recorded as "beginning at the northeast corner of the intersection of Speed and Spottswood . . . " It was described as the almost-five acres previously bought in 1869 for $1,117.50 by Shelton R. White from Matilda and Pembroke A. Brawner. The Brawners bought the property from John Speed, Trustee for Janette Spottswood and her husband Edwin A. Spottswood in 1868. The trust for the property was described in the marriage contract between Edwin Spottswood and Janette Armour (?) in 1862.

The literary society had formed to present plays and incorporated to buy the property for establishing a theatre. As the area recovered from the Civil War, rebounded from the 1873 yellow fever epedimic, and settled into a growth mode, it seemed a time for cultural associations to move from inside the city limits to the rapidly populating suburbs.

Cancellation of public meetings during the horrendous epidemic of 1878 resulted in economic deprivation for the Cliosophic group. Lack of support from either local or City residents caused the Society to default on its mortgage loan. Foreclosure resulted, with the property auctioned on the steps of the court house in March 1880.

St. John's began the decade as a parish. By the end of the 1870s, both the city of Memphis and St. John's had relinquished their status.

On January 31, 1879 the City of Memphis ceased to exist, relinquishing its charter.

Mission Becomes a Parish

5

The Church Home that Sister Hughetta had visited just after it opened stayed in the Buntyn area during 1870-71. It eventually returned to the outlying area, and the chapel was later a mission of St. John's. Meanwhile, the little church suffered numerous setbacks. A newspaper account says that St. John's burned in 1875—probably the second time it had been devastated by fire. From the clues it is clear that St. John's was an established parish.

Public Ledger, Tuesday, May 22, 1877
On tomorrow evening at the Bethel Place, on the Pidgeon (sic) Roost road, some four miles from the city, the ladies of St. John's Parish (Episcopal) will give a festival party for the purpose of raising funds with which to aid in the erection of a church.

On the day of the party the newspaper invitation was even more enticing.

Public Ledger, Wednesday, May 23, 1877
A pleasant moonlight drive this evening of four miles out on the Pidgeon Roost road will carry you to the old Bethel place, well known to old residents for the beauty and picturesqueness of its surroundings. A fete champetre will be held there from 5 to 10 o'clock p.m. today, by the ladies of that vicinity, proceeds to be donated to St. John's (Episcopal) parish to assist them in rebuilding their church, burned during the war. Price of admission, 25¢; refreshments, 25¢. Memphians will find this a very different affair from the hot and dusty city picnics to which they are accustomed, and it is hoped they will lend their assistance toward making this a good old fashioned enjoyable occasion.

The Bethell mansion, built by Colonel Pinckney C. Bethell, was 4 1/2 miles from Court Square. Colonel Bethell, father of William D. Bethell, bought the land in 1858. The Colonel was reputed to be perhaps the wealthiest man in the pre-war South. When the City of Memphis reverted to taxing district status, Colonel Bethell was among the business leaders who advocated that merchants pay their taxes in advance so the government could work. He proposed that 50 men pay $1,000 each in advance taxes to fund improvements to sanitation and streets.

Pat Meath bought the Bethell house and 176 acres in 1866 for $125,000—an amount that evidently generated incredulous gossip, at least for newspapers. When Meath defaulted, Bethell had to buy back the mortgage. A Mrs. Wheeler later bought it for $11,000.

P. C. Bethell's son, W. D. Bethell, married a niece of General Gideon Pillow. He moved back to Memphis in the 1880s and became president of State National Bank that later became First Tennessee Bank.

The 1870s were another difficult decade, while the little mission struggled for footing. The land boom of the 1850s was followed by the Civil War, wiping out much of the benefits realized by connections of the railroad. Even Calvary had no delegates to some Conventions in the 1850s-60s. The Diocesan Journal was not even published for 1861-65. Then the depression that struck in 1873 lasted an unprecedented 66 months, finally ending just as the third epidemic of yellow fever hit. And fire was a major hazard for the volatile wood structures illuminated by candles or gas light.

The parish was admitted to the Diocese in 1871—probably for the second time. Convention records show that in the Report of the Committee on New Parishes, St. John's was granted an exception of waiting two more weeks to fulfill the canonical requirement of three months' formal notice to the Bishop. This would indicate that it was not new, but re-applying. The recommendation was adopted and it was admitted. Lay delegates to the 1871 convention were Edmund D. Bray (who had represented Calvary Church 30 years previously), Henry E. Cannon, and Levi Jay. Peter Wager was ordained as a deacon that same year, with the ordination service at St. John's.

St. John's Buntyn was assessed $40 by the Diocese in 1871.

In 1872, The Rev. Mr. Peter Wager was Deacon-in-Charge of St. John's, Buntyn and of Otey Chapel, Shelby County. The report for that year was by Treasurer, Levi Jay.

The following year, the report was submitted by Peter Wager, Deacon-in-Charge, with a report for the Church Orphan's Home also submitted by him as Chaplain.

Peter Wager had served on the Vestry of St. Mary's, and was superintendent of Sunday School at the Church of the Good Shepherd. It was there that he met Emma Woods, another Sunday School teacher. They married and had five children. He served missions in Memphis, then went as Rector to a parish in Florence, Alabama, before returning to Memphis.

In 1874, following the year of the 1873 yellow fever epidemic, no one was listed from St. John's. The report to the Diocese shows that the parish was $48 in arrears, and was assessed an additional $23. The next year was similar, with a greater deficit. There were no clergy in the report, and the parish was $71 in arrears. And in 1876, there was no mention.

The daily *Memphis Evening Herald* began in the spring of 1877 and cost $.50 per month—and only lasted for eight months. County scrip was selling at $.95-$.96. Gold was 102 1/4 on January 1. Deerskins and coonskins ranged from $.18 to $.50. Low Middling sold for 10 3/8. The world's population was estimated at 1,396,752,000, with 685,450, 411 (49%) under Christian government. It was a summer of record rainfall in Memphis.

The Deacon-in-Charge at St. John's, Peter Wager, was ordained as priest that year. St. John's report to the Annual Convention was submitted by John D. Huhn, Secretary-Treasurer, whose address was #12, Jefferson Street, Memphis (no explanation of why he lived so far away).

Mr. Huhn reported to the Diocese that:

In explanation of the meagreness of the accompanying

report, the Secretary of St. John's Parish desires to state that since the destruction by fire of the chapel attached to the Church Home at Buntyn Station, the Parish has had no permanent place for services and gradually became quite disorganized. The books and papers were either destroyed by fire or lost, and there is no ready method by which a perfectly accurate report could be made out.

During the fall the use of the Grande Hall near Shelby County Fair Grounds was obtained for alternate Sunday afternoons, and since then, with the kindly and faithful aid of the Rev. Messrs. White, Parsons, Harris, and Gee of the Memphis Convocation, seconded by a timely and very welcome visit from the Honored Bishop of the Diocese, the Parish has been making good progress.

On April 15, under the guidance of the Rev. George C. Harris, a meeting of the communicants of the Parish was held, and a Vestry elected and organized and this resolution of scattered elements into a tangible shape has aroused a hopeful feeling in our small circle of faithful that we feel sure will, with continued assistance from the Memphis Clergy, result in still further advance toward a position of usefulness.

The erection of a church building has now the anxious consideration of the Vestry, and we hope before the next annual Convention to have at least established some line of policy which may eventuate in the consummation of our earnest desire to place St. John's Parish upon a firm and lasting basis.

> *- John D. Huhn, Sec'ty.*
> *#12 Jefferson St.*
> *Memphis, Tn.*

The Rev. Mr. Peter Wager

No priest is mentioned in the 1878 report, and lay delegates listed were absent from the convention. Listed were Henry E. Cannon, Calhoun Cannon, and John D. Huhn. The Parochial Report listed the church as "St. John's, Shelby County," with four ministers who had served one to three times during the year. Mr. Huhn, Lay-Reader-in-Charge who submitted the report, stated that 35 services had been held during the year by the Lay Reader.

There was no report for 1879.

Mr. Huhn's report in 1880 lists no priest or lay people, but does report remodeling of the building. His report from the *Journal of Convention*:

> *Remarks*: From date of last Report, two years ago, services have been held only sixteen times—the last on Sept. 1, 1878. We have had the services of a clergyman but once during these two years, viz: on May 1, 1878, when Rev. George White, D.D., baptized an infant and celebrated the Holy Communion. The yellow fever deprived us of our place of worship. We have, nevertheless, not relaxed our efforts for the Church, and have just concluded the purchase of an eligible building in Buntyn, which we are now remodeling.
>
> - *John D. Hughn, Lay-Reader*

Despite the enigmatic clues as to the previous two years (and the variant spelling of his name), Mr. Hughn's report seems to tie together some loose threads in the tapestry of St. John's history. The summer of 1878 brought the tragic epidemic that shut down public meetings for months and changed interaction between the city of Memphis and outlying country communities. At the end of that period, it is likely from extant records that it was the property at Semmes and Spottswood that was purchased. It's difficult to verify, but it would seem that the "old church" was actually the church before it was owned by the Cliosophic Society, then again bought as the church when the Cliosophic Society was bankrupt.

In *A History of St. John's Parish*, written in 1938 by Mrs. Elizabeth Saunders Ramsay, the story of how the church acquired the building is as follows:

"Then, on September 1, 1877, the property, lot, and building, which has been used as a mission, was sold by Colonel Shelton R. White for $37.50 to the Cliosophic Society. This Society was incorporated July 18, 1877, of that

"The yellow fever deprived us of our place of worship. We have, nevertheless, not relaxed our efforts for the Church..."

purpose, as set forth in their charter, 'of cultivating a correct and refined taste for literature and social enjoyment.' The incorporators of the society were W. D. Lumpkin, Calhoun Cannon, John R. Greer, Junius Greene, Thomas J. Humphreys, and it is interesting to note that the witness of this contract was George B. Peters, Jr., father of Mrs. Charles N. Burch. Under its president, James M. Richardson, the Cliosophic Society carried out its purpose by staging Shakespearean dramas, roles being taken by members of the society, among them many Episcopalians actively interested in carrying on the work at St. John's mission. It is said that the society permitted the building to be used as a church on Sunday whenever it was possible to get a minister to come to Buntyn, but it was a short-lived venture, for the next year, on May 18, 1878, the Cliosophic Literary Society borrowed $200, naming Mr. Walter Gregory as trustee in the trust deed to secure the payment of the loan and putting up the property and building as collateral. The society was unable to meet its debt, the creditor was forced to foreclose, and Mr. Gregory had to offer the property for sale to the highest bidder.

"Mrs. Tom Watkins, Sr., recalls the day Judge Sneed came to tell her husband that the property was advertized for sale. 'Have you got any money in your pocket?' he asked Dr. Watkins, and the answer was, about 10 dollars. The two of them set off for the auction sale on Tuesday, the 9th day of March, 1880. The transaction is recorded in the Register's Office . . . 'whereas the Cliosophic Literary Society has defaulted on the loan and whereas this property has been advertized for sale for 30 days . . . I have sold same for $270 to the highest bidder, John L. T. Sneed, as agent and trustee of St. John Parish, Protestant Episcopal Church of said County of Shelby, State of Tennessee . . . I do hereby bargain, convey, and sell to him to be held, kept and controlled by him as an Episcopal Chapel for worship of Almighty God, but for no secular purpose whatever until same can be

Judge John L.T. Sneed

remodelled and made ready for consecration when the said John L. T. Sneed is to convey the same for like purposes to the Protestant Episcopal Diocese of the State of Tennessee.'

"Mr. Elam, father of Mrs. Laura Sharpe, and his brother, John, went to work to transform the hall into a church. They built the vestibule, placed the wooden cross on the front, and shaped up the chancel, doing much of the work themselves. Calvary Parish of Memphis gave the wood railing and lectern to the new church. . . . [However] . . . there was no minister, rectors coming out from Memphis on the train to the little church in Buntyn."

There was no new space added until 1917, except for a small room built onto the south side of the building for Mr. Stewart, a Scotsman who held services even if Mrs. Laura Sharpe was the only communicant. Both he and Mrs. Sharpe loved flowers and gardened in order to keep flowers on the altar. Mr. Stewart died and the mission was without a regular pastor for a few years prior to re-calling The Rev. Mr. Wager in 1897.

In the years that the parish grew, Judge Sneed did not transfer the deed

to St. John's—probably because the church was not incorporated. When St. John's wanted to sell the property to the East Memphis Lions Club, after the church moved to the new building, the title problem was discovered. Mr. T. K. Robinson received the property as Trustee, and gave it to the Diocese, who returned title to St. John's.

Despite having property for St. John's Parish to build a church, there was no report of delegates or clergy to the 1881 Convention.

Mission Status Again

6

The 1880s were grim years for Memphis. Following the yellow fever epidemic in 1878, the city lost its charter.

There was still a faithful group at St. John's in 1882. The report to the Annual Convention listed the number of communicants as 27. There was no report for the next three years, although "St. John's Buntyn" was assessed $2 at the convention in 1885.

Judge John L.T. Sneed's name appears in the 1886 report, when he was listed as a mission lay person for St. John's Chapel, Buntyn.

...many of the old families in the Buntyn area remained, helping to carry the crippled city toward new strength.

With loss of the city charter, Memphis became a taxing district, not to regain city status for 14 years. Although much of the wealth left the city during the dark decades of 1860-1880, many of the old families in the Buntyn area remained, helping to carry the crippled city toward new strength. One of the debt commissioners for the taxing district, appointed by Gov. Marks, was P. C. Bethell—at whose lavish home the benefit for St. John's was held just the summer before the most tragic yellow fever epidemic.

Reports for the years 1887 to 1889 show no clergy and no lay representatives at the Annual Convention.

However, St. John's was assessed $10 in 1888, and paid it.

The little group reorganized in 1889, and a benefit held at the residence of W. N. Hunt on Central was organized to raise money for a new church.

Although there was no church in 1889, The Rev. Mr. Charles Stewart is listed as Priest-in-Charge of the mission. He was still listed in 1890-91, but did not attend the conventions. The mission was still paying assessments, however.

St. John's does not appear in Convention records again for seven years. Finally, on September 12, 1897, Mr. Stewart was succeeded by The Rev. Mr. Peter Wager, who was recalled in March 1897, and "commenced services to St. John's Buntyn," which was still listed as a mission. Under his long and able guidance the membership increased. In 1898 the building was dedicated as a mission for the worship of God, in accordance with the provisions of the deed of sale to Judge Sneed.

Mr. Wager noted in his diary in 1901 that there were then 37 communicants and a very good Sunday School, in which both his daughters taught. But a few years later, the congregation drifted off again, this time, so the story goes, because the residents of Buntyn preferred to go into the big Memphis churches, since the street car tracks now reached as far as the Country Club. In the fall of 1907, when Mr. and Mrs. Lehman Johnson with their four-year-old daughter, Mary, moved to Buntyn, Mrs. Laura Sharpe was the only communicant, and in very bad weather Mr. Wager would come to Mrs. Sharpe's home and there conduct the Sunday church service. Mrs. Johnson, a musician, played the little hand-pumped organ.

The next spring, Mr. and Mrs. Harry Ramsay and their two small sons, Jack and Harry, Jr., moved to Buntyn and immediately transferred their memberships from Calvary Parish to St. John's.

When the Ramsays came to St. John's in 1908, that made three families who comprised the membership: the Lehman Johnsons and daughter, Mary; the L.C. Sharpes; the Ramsays, and their collie, Bobby. The dog was very faithful in attendance, and would lie down by the pot-bellied stove in the one-room building.

The Rev. Mr. Peter Wager

Mr. Tate, the priest in charge, came for dinner with the Ramsays every Sunday. He was a very large man and broke so many chairs that Mrs. Ramsay began to bring in a kitchen chair for him, saying that she was not going to mend any more chairs, and she was not going to embarrass him again.

In 1912 the congregation further increased by the arrival of Mr. and Mrs. Palmer Farnsworth and their three sons, Minter, Bethel, and Palmer, Jr. Mrs. Farnsworth led in singing the hymns, while Mrs. Johnson played the organ. There was no vestry; Mr. Farnsworth and Mr. Ramsay took turns collecting the offering.

Records for many years are missing—due primarily to fires that destroyed them. But there are minutes of meetings of St. John's Branch of the Woman's Auxiliary from 1916 until modern history began with The Rev. Mr. Alfred Loaring-Clark.

There is only slight mention of World War I; most of the items in the 1916-19 minutes relate to the Parish.

Organized again in late 1916, St. John's Branch of the Woman's Auxiliary met faithfully, even when there were only three or four women attending regularly. Mrs. Clark Coe was elected president. The Rev. Mr. Grant Knoft usually opened and closed the meetings with devotional services. The women corresponded with "Mrs. Loaring-Clark in Chattanooga . . . and Mrs. DuBose of Sewanee" about study materials and mission projects. In November 1916 the little group read the Constitution and By-Laws of Calvary Branch of the Auxiliary, to better understand the structure of the organization.

For as in Adam all die, even so in Christ shall all be made alive.   1 Cor. 15. 22.

Given to Elizabeth Williams by The Rev. Mr. Peter Wager, Easter, 1914

Interiors of Church at Semmes and Spottswood

Ada Loaring-Clark

December 21, 1916 - Minutes of the Woman's Auxiliary

. . . Mrs. Knoft resigned as Sec., at this meeting, but said that she would write the minutes. This she failed to do. I was elected Sec. and have written what I could remember, which isn't much after a lapse of nearly four months. I have a distinct recollection of how intensely cold it was, and that perhaps accounted for the very slim attendance. There were only five members present - Mrs. Farnsworth, Mrs. Coe, Mrs. Knoft, Mrs. Phillips, and Miss Phillips. . .The President instructed me to send one dollar to this cause (in South Dakota) out of the funds on hand so that leaves one dollar and twenty cents in the Treasury.

-*Anna P. Phillips, Sec.*

In July 1917 Mrs. Willins and Mrs. Woolwine joined the group.

"It was a beautiful morning, which perhaps in some measure accounted for our unusually large attendance. . . . We were glad indeed to add to our roll Mrs. Willins and Mrs. Woolwine. We are so few in numbers, that two new members at one meeting are more than welcome."

Woman's Auxiliary -
St. John's Church -

Record of N. T. O.
from 1918 to and
including 1930 -

1918	9.14
1919	12.75
1920	25.00
1921	50.00
1922	42.55
1923	43.52
1924	57.53
1925	52.50
1926	52.38
1927	48.55
1928	100.84
1929	106.91
1930	93.74

They met in homes, on porches, at the church, on Mrs. Farnsworth's lawn "with her beautiful flowers in the background," and later created a special room at the church for meetings. Dues were 10 cents each per month. They also gave money to United Offering boxes and the Contingent Fund. They contributed to Diocesan missions, the General Mission fund, and to special mission appeals. By May 1917, following a talk by The Rev. Dr. Bennett, the group agreed that they would double the pledge, giving $10 to General Missions and $10 to Diocesan Missions.

That September, Mrs. Ragland came, saying she would attend when she was in Buntyn. In October the group wanted to pay the pledge to the Diocese for missions, but collected only $9.45. Miss Phillips wrote that, "I supplied what was necessary to make the $10.00."

"We hope to have Mr. Williams [The Rev. Mr. Paul N. Williams] with us often, for we are very much in need of helpful, intelligent instruction about the work of the Auxiliary."

At Mr. Williams' suggestion, the United Offering was added to the plate collection, and the Women joyfully reported sending $21 to the United Offering fund.

When Mrs. Coe resigned as President in April 1919, "very much to the regret of every member," Mrs. Ramsay was elected.

In June 1920, Mrs. Glover made 17 members. Although Mr. Williams recommended that the Auxiliary take the summer off, they voted to continue with the July and August meetings as usual. "There was much talk, as usual, as to things that might, could, would, or should be done but I do not think we came to any definite decisions."

December 18, 1930

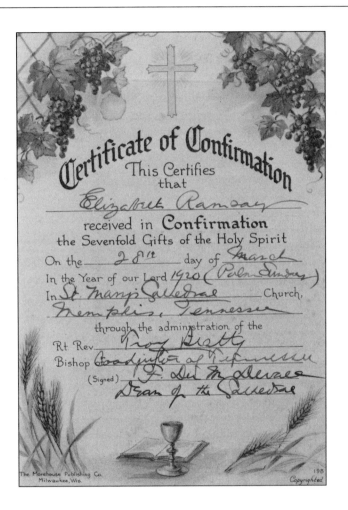

In 1920, when the Scrivener clan moved to Buntyn, the 14 new persons almost doubled the membership. Certainly, the four children more than doubled the youth group. Already there were the Ramsays, the Palmer Farnsworths, the Woolwines, the Verdels, the Dorseys, and Mrs. Laura Sharpe. Mrs. Sharpe's lovingly tended yard stretched from the church grounds north for the entire block, up to Rutland's General Store and the Buntyn Post Office, which occupied the corner at Semmes and Southern.

The Woman's Auxiliary united with The Woman's Guild in October 1920, calling the new organization The Church Service League. Officers elected were: Mrs. Dabney, President; Mrs. Sharpe, Vice President; Mrs. Franklin, Secretary; Mrs. Coe, Treasurer; Mrs. Ramsay, Chairman of Guild; and Mrs. Robinson, Chairman of Auxiliary. Mrs. Randall was elected Choir Mother.

January 1921 brought Mrs. Dorsey and Mrs. Scrivener. Mrs. Robinson was unanimously chosen as the delegate to the Convention to be held at Calvary. (Prior to the Diocesan Convention in 1951 the Clergy and Lay Delegates [men] and the Women of the Church met as one Convention.)

The women took as a project paying for painting the floor, wainscoting, and pews. They bought carpet and planted shrubs. They dusted the sanctuary after the church had been cleaned by the sexton. They paid for laundering the choir cottas and made new caps and cassocks. They served supper to the Brotherhood on October 30, 1920. They made altar linens, sewed for the needy, and sent children's clothes to the Church Home. They earned $7.80 from a musicale and $30.30 from a Valentine's party. They sold bazaar items and sent missionary barrels, organized a Church Periodic (sic) Club (bringing magazines to send to others) and Daughters of the King, took Stereopticon pictures to Mary Galloway Home, visited the Home for Incurables and Crippled Children's Hospital, bought window screens, sent a book to St. Paul's College Library in Tokyo, donated to the Traveler's Aid Society, discussed the "difficult problems of the playground," and talked about having a lawn party as a fund raiser. They earned $.76 per month interest from the bank on their account

> **Mrs. Dabney brought to the attention of the group "the necessity of having some place where the young folks of the Church could meet in the afternoons for games and recreation, where they would be properly chaperoned."**

and made money on their cookbook—sold for $1 each. Proceeds from cookbook sales paid for painting the exterior of the church. Mrs. Ragland wrote from Marianna, Arkansas, sending her love and money.

In the summer of 1921, Mrs. Dabney brought to the attention of the group "the necessity of having some place where the young folks of the Church could meet in the afternoons for games and recreation, where they would be properly chaperoned." After considerable discussion, it was agreed that the Service League's room at the church would be opened on weekdays from 2:30 until 5:00 for the remainder of summer vacation. Their goal was to create a community center, "and that the movement will be productive of much good."

November 18, 1921 - Minutes

"Refreshments were served by Miss Harrison and Mrs. Woolwine. The nut bread and chocolate were delicious and those of you who were absent can just imagine what you missed."

Earnings in 1922 were $46.50 from the Halloween Party, $115.89 from the Christmas Bazaar, and $30.38 from cookbook sales—in addition to dues, offerings, and miscellaneous small sums. When Bishop Gailor wrote that only $60 would support an Armenian child for a year, they adopted one child.

Although the records were apparently among those burned in the fire at the Loaring-Clark's library, there was also a Vestry in 1922. The Service League asked the Vestry to pay half of the $10 for flowers sent to Bishop Beatty's funeral; the Vestry paid the entire amount.

Mr. and Mrs. Tate attended the November 1922 meeting of the Service League. After a "rising vote of thanks. . . to Mrs. Lowrance and Mrs. Lewis and those who helped

> **"...The nut bread and chocolate were delicious and those of you who were absent can just imagine what you missed."**

them with the work on the church windows," the meeting focused on needs for the church. The women wanted to buy a new organ, but discussed the $700 debt on the church and that the Vestry had no funds to meet the $100 due to the Nation Wide Campaign. In 1923, they made a second payment of $25 on the organ and sent money in support of St. Agnes School in Tokyo.

February 1, 1924 - Minutes

"Several were asked to accept the Secretaryship but declined, so Mrs. Farnsworth, being absent, was unanimously elected."

By 1924 the meeting place for the Service League is called "Wager Hall." The Bazaar that year netted $84.47. The Episcopal churches were in charge of one week's lunches served to attendees of the Billy Sunday campaign in May 1924. Five members of St. John's offered to help; others volunteered to make cakes the church was asked to donate.

Exterior of St. John's at Semmes and Spottswood

The events in 1925 were disparate, but notable to the group. They bought a purple stole for The Rev. Mr. Martin Luther Tate. They bought ice cream from Clover Farm Dairy for an interparochial ice cream social. They sold cookbooks and old magazines, bought cups and saucers, paint, sewing materials, and flowers for funerals. And they organized a Garden Mart in 1925—netting an unprecedented $154.76.

The following year they made even more money: a net of $348.65 and had $150 in a "time deposit due in June," which earned $6. In addition to the very profitable Garden Mart, they sold calendars and handicrafts, bought Easter lilies, altar candles, Sunday School books, cleaning and food supplies, and *Popular Mechanics* for the Church Periodical Club. Mrs. Shawhan's phone number (7-3061) and Mrs. Farnsworth's number (2-7265) were often busy.

Then came the Crash. In the boom years of 1922-1929, it seemed that the economy, despite an uneven growth rate, was moving into mature industrial security. By 1929, the automobile industry took first place in manufacturing, both in terms of value and of value added. There were 2,798,737 passenger cars manufactured in 1929. Also, plastics (especially rayon textiles), refrigerators, and gas production rose.

On October 24, 13 million shares of stock changed hands, followed by trades of 16 million shares five days later. By November 13, losses wiped out about $30-billion in market value, and it rose to $75-billion by mid-1932.

St. John's first rector came just before the stock market crash. The Rev. Mr. Alfred Loaring-Clark had been missioner for St. Alban's as well as St. John's, but, after he became Rector for St. John's, the St. Alban's mission was changed to the care of the Dean of Convocation on November 7, 1930.

Ben Shawhan, Treasurer during the financial crises of 1929 to 1934, told that it was not unusual to find a red tag on the water meter reading "Cut off; bill unpaid." The 60 contributors struggled to keep the small church alive. At the Vestry meeting in February 1940, The Rev. Mr. Loaring-Clark reminded the members that, through that period, the "coal company carried us along, as Bill Woolwine's father could well testify, the light and gas companies were lenient, the missionaries received our dab of money months late, and sometimes the Rector went unpaid."

Buntyn was incorporated into the city in 1929.

*There was a young cleric so glib
Who, forgetting the tune, would ad lib;
His people, in terror, would swear by his error,
This Padre so base is called "Tib."*

–R.W.

Looking at the snapshots, you see the character of the parish. There were always families, and food, and flowers, and fun. Smiling people made parties at the church. But Alfred Joseph Loaring-Clark, fondly called "Tib" by his friends, came as rector to the newly designated parish just as the Depression changed lifestyles.

It's clear from his writings: He was in many ways a visionary. A man who would have led the marches during the turbulent '60s. A man who would have embraced the global village as "my dear people." Yet a man who was truly a leader for one of the most dynamic Episcopal parishes in Tennessee during the turmoil of a major depression and world war. He must have been a man that people adored or totally differed with in ideology. And he left giant footprints.

Alfred Loaring-Clark was born in London, England, in 1900, a son of The Rev. Dr. William James Loaring-Clark and his wife Ada. He attended Baylor School in Chattanooga, took his B.A. at the University of Chattanooga, and

"Tib"

his B.D. at Sewanee. He was ordained to the diaconate and the priesthood in 1926 by Bishop Gailor and served as Canon Missioner at St. Mary's Cathedral from 1926 to 1928, and as vicar of St. Alban's Mission from 1926 to 1929. He became the first rector of St. John's Episcopal Church

And he left giant footprints.

in October 1928, just as St. John's was emerging from decades of upheaval and mission status to again have the status of a small and struggling parish. Records from St. Mary's say that it was the third time they had revived St. John's parish when Mr. Loaring-Clark was sent to the mission.

He looked as if he had stepped out of a Scott Fitzgerald novel, or a Noel Coward play. He held a cigarette or tennis racquet at just the right angle. He was dapper, brilliant, and ahead of his time in social consciousness, like a 1960s activist decades too soon.

How he came to be a U.S. citizen would not be believable as fiction. His father, a Londoner, was studying medicine. One day, as he delivered a paper on medical ethics at the Speaker's Corner, the Bishop of Missouri happened to walk by, and stopped to listen. After the speech he introduced himself to the speaker, saying, "Young man, you're in the wrong field. If you should ever decide to go into the ministry instead, come to the United States and I would be glad to sponsor you." So Loaring-Clark talked with his wife, Ada, and they packed up the children, and "Cousin Lucy" who came to help with them, and moved from London to Missouri. In Missouri, Dr. Loaring-Clark

The Rt. Rev. William Augustus Jones, Jr.

studied under the Bishop, then served as an evangelist to various missions. He became rector at St. Paul's in Chattanooga. When his wife, who was just as active in church work, became diabetic, her doctor prescribed that she must slow down. The Bishop of Tennessee asked The Rev. Dr. Loaring-Clark to help out with a floundering church in Jackson, Tennessee, where quarters were provided in the New South Hotel, giving Mrs. Loaring-Clark relief from household duties.

Young Alfred wanted to run away and join the Royal Canadian Air Force as a World War I aviator. He was a student at the University of Chattanooga, but only 17, he was too young to enlist in the United States Armed Forces. Finally, his parents consented, reluctantly, and he left Tennessee for Toronto. War ended before he was in combat. However, his brother's death made him a sincere advocate of peace.

Returning to the university, he earned a Bachelor of Arts degree in 1921. After two years on faculty at Baylor Military Academy in Chattanooga, he returned to school and earned a Bachelor of Divinity degree from the University of the South at Sewanee in 1926. He was ordained by Bishop Thomas F. Gailor on August 24, 1926.

Alfred Loaring-Clark married Margaret Lee Austin on September 29, 1926 in the Methodist Church in Smithfield, North Carolina. By 1930, they had two daughters, Margaret Ada and Sarah Austin. (Interestingly, Margaret married William Augustus Jones, Jr., who was the Bishop of Missouri, until retirement.)

For two years after coming to Memphis he served as assistant to the dean at St. Mary's Cathedral and as a

> *Dean Noe came in and the young priest said to him, "I have my sermon ready." The Dean asked, "Do you know it?" Mr. Loaring-Clark replied, "Yes." Dean Noe took the sermon, tore it up, and told Mr. Loaring-Clark to preach it from his heart.*

circuit rider to missions in West Tennessee, becoming the regular priest for St. Alban's in South Memphis and missions in Woodstock and Covington.

After ordination, he was assigned to the staff of St. Mary's Cathedral as Canon Missioner. Ordained on Tuesday, his first sermon was scheduled for the following Sunday at the 11 o'clock morning prayer service. For his first

The Rev. Mr. Alfred Joseph Loaring-Clark

time to occupy the Cathedral pulpit, he took as the subject "Ye shall know the truth and the truth shall make you free." Ellen Correll, who for many decades worked in Christian Education at the Cathedral, told the story that, on Saturday morning before he was to preach his first sermon at the Cathedral, The Rev. Mr. Loaring-Clark came into her office and said, "I have my sermon ready." Dean Noe came in and the young priest said to him, "I have my sermon ready." The Dean asked, "Do you know it?" Mr. Loaring-Clark replied, "Yes." Dean Noe took the sermon, tore it up, and told Mr. Loaring-Clark to preach it from his heart.

Reports in the few extant records show that he was earnest in his endeavors as a circuit rider to the missions. The vestrymen of St. John's requested that ". . . the Bishop of the Diocese assign Alfred Loaring-Clark to St. John's Protestant Episcopal Church, Buntyn, Tennessee effective March 1, 1928 until October 1, 1928, at a salary of $125 per month, [while] the committee continues efforts to secure a permanent rector for the church." The "assignment" lasted for almost 25 years, as the growing parish found a match with the young clergyman.

The Loaring-Clarks made their home in a city that had the reputation as the most vice-ridden city in the nation during the 1920s. Memphis was notorious for the number of murders, and its reputation nationally was that of a dangerous river town. As the political regime cracked down, the city became more tenable, under the tolerances cited in the song, "Mr. Crump Don't 'llow." The Roaring Twenties frenzies quieted as disaster followed disaster during the 1930s.

To the young Loaring-Clarks, the decade began joyously. The young Rector's wife celebrated the new baby's birth with a poem.

To Margaret Ada

You came to me, a part
Of God's own heart—
And in my gratitude
I felt unworthy of the task
Which now was mine.

I wished for you
Bright Joy,
And Cheer,
And Happiness unending;
A Courage strong,
A love for Truth,
Your life in service spending.

And oh, my baby, fervently I pray
That clear and shining
You keep the pathway back to Him
His guidance ever finding.
  – *Margaret Lee Austin Loaring-Clark 1/4/30*

The beautiful young mother was diagnosed with tuberculosis and, shortly after the birth of her second daughter, Sarah, she went to a hospital in Asheville, North Carolina, leaving her baby with her parents. The poem for this baby, whom she had seen only once, was different.

Sarah

They say you turn your big blue eyes
First one way—then the other
And look around, as if to say,
"Now just Where is my Mother?"

Your Mother's in the mountains, Sarah
Getting well and strong
So she can come and play with you,
And sing you little songs.

Oh we're so very lucky
To have your dear Mamo
Who's loving you and watching you
And helping you to grow.

Sarah, stay out in the Sun
And laugh and kick and coo,
Then some fine day your Mother
Will be coming home to you.

The sad young rector commuted between North Carolina and Memphis for months, trying to keep an eye on both his personal family and his parish family. She died from pneumonia, a complication from the tuberculosis. With the help of "Miss Lucy" Cochran, who helped to rear three generations of Loaring-Clark children, the young rector managed his church and family. "Miss Lucy" lived in Memphis her last 16 years, and was eulogized in the newspaper when she died here in 1945.

Connie Austin recalls that Mr. Loaring-Clark was Memphis' most eligible bachelor for a few years, included in many social gatherings, beloved by his parishioners and friends. He was listed among attendees at many social events written up by society columns in the newspapers. When he began dating Mrs. Clara Cocke Maer, a teacher at St. Mary's School, they often went to dinner and bridge games with the John Austins. Sometimes on moonlight nights the four of them took quiet drives in the Austins' car. The Rev. Mr. Loaring-Clark and Mrs. Maer married in July 1938, and the new Mrs. Loaring-Clark brought her daughter, Clara, to the old frame Victorian rectory on the corner of Southern and Goodwyn.

The congregation grew from 75 to 400 in The Rev. Mr. Loaring-Clark's first eight years as Rector at St. John's.

The Loaring-Clarks buying a ticket to an operetta from Helen Shawhan

Lawrence Scrivener and Margaret, Clara and Sarah at the "Old Rectory," 1940

Parishioners thanked him for his decision in 1935 to decline a call to Christ Episcopal Church in Raleigh, North Carolina. And the parish continued to grow.

Newspaper reprints (1939) of his texts confirm the very literate quality of his sermons:

Christianity has often displayed amazing versatility. Victorious lives are found in the slums and on Fifth Avenue, in academic circles and in arduous task. Robert Browning never knew the meaning of want and Shakespeare hardly ever escaped it. John Bunyan wrote his most glorious work while a prisoner in Ludgate jail, and St. Francis of Assisi lived and sang under the blue Mediterranean sky.

One would say then that in this matter of victorious living, not outward circumstances, but inward light, is the determining factor. These are qualities in the Christ-centered life which never can be produced without Him.

He was something of a Renaissance Man, and everything of a social activist whose conscience made the whole city his parish. As the arbiter of two garment firm strikes in 1937, his negotiation was called by a fellow minister "the most outstanding piece of work ever rendered by a Memphis clergyman in the field of industrial relations." During the strike Mayor Crump telephoned Loaring-Clark to ask, "Why don't you mind your own business?" Mr. Loaring-Clark replied that "It is my business. The task of the Church is to attempt to reconcile man with man." He later received a letter from Mr. Crump thanking him for his compassion.

One would say then that in this matter of victorious living, not outward circumstances, but inward light, is the determining factor.

The Rev. Mr. Loaring-Clark was chairman of the Social Justice Committee of the Memphis Ministers' Association, President in 1938-39. He was President of Civitan Club in 1931. He enjoyed piloting a Waco plane and was known then as the city's first "flying parson." Later activities—usually with parishioners—included fishing, duck hunting, and golf. He enjoyed swimming

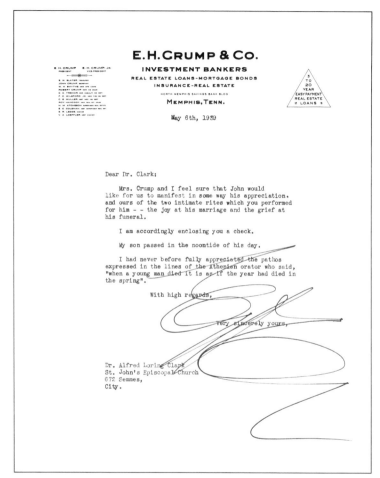

May 6, 1939

and tennis, he sang and played violin, he was a student of psychology, literature, and science as well as theology. He wrote poetry, starred in Memphis Little Theatre's production of "On Borrowed Time," and served as chaplain for the Episcopal students at what is now University of Memphis. In addition to his parish duties he worked with Boy Scout groups, many civic and welfare drives, and women incarcerated at the penal farm.

He was Director of Youth Service Bureau, served on the recreational committee of Memphis and Shelby County Community Council. He was highly praised for his work during the flood of 1937 when refugees crowded the Fairgrounds and Auditorium. Untiring in efforts to obtain milk and other supplies, he offered comfort and aid to victims.

Tenant farming, begun in this country in 1613—only six years after the settlement of Jamestown—increased markedly in cotton-producing areas, with tenancy increasing from 26% of total farms in 1880 to 42.2% by 1935. But the wholesale price index of farm products dropped with the Depression. The Rev. Mr. Loaring-Clark took a progressive stand for improvement of agricultural labor conditions in the South, better housing, and abolition of child labor. A newspaper article dated September 28, 1935 recounts his reply to President Roosevelt's request for "counsel and advice" of clergymen throughout the nation. The Rev. Mr. Loaring-Clark's letter to the president challenged the U.S. government to do something to remedy the tenant farmer situation in the south. Yet he did not condemn either owners or workers, only the system. He wrote that "It is stupid to condemn [share-croppers] as idle, shiftless, and immoral . . . [when they are] the product of a vicious, stifling environment." But he did not put the blame on landowners, "by no means scoundrels or selfish task-masters. One may not fairly condemn individuals for the evils which exist." In July 1937 the Bankhead-Jones Farm Tenant Act established the Farm Security Administration, to provide low-interest loans for tenants to purchase land.

From newspaper articles and from reminiscences of his parishioners, it seems clear that The Rev. Mr. Loaring-Clark was able to espouse controversial issues without dividing his congregation—by the sheer magnetism of his personality. His warmth and leadership allowed him to extend his influence far beyond the bounds of his parish. The letter to President Roosevelt concluded that "economic programs lie beyond the field for which [the clergy] have been trained; theirs is not the task of creating the details of a new economic order but rather to '[show] the . . . consequences [of injustice] and throw the challenge to evolve patiently and intelligently a new and better system'."

In today's parlance, it could be said that he "walked the talk." No empty rhetoric of the "Do as I say" variety was ever evident in his words. From sermons, Vestry minutes, newspaper accounts, and parish reminiscences

"...One may not fairly condemn individuals for the evils which exist."

it is obvious that he believed passionately in the Gospel message he saw revealed, and that he dearly loved his congregation.

On May 30, 1932 he offered to the Vestry that they reduce his salary by whatever amount they thought best to relieve the financial difficulties of the church brought on by the Depression. They decided upon $40 per month.

He spoke at literary clubs, Rotary, ecumenical services at the Overton Park Shell, music clubs, men's clubs, civic clubs, church gatherings of many denominations, Memphis State athletic events, Southwestern.

Elected to several important committees at 1934 annual Diocesan Convention, he was alternate Deputy to

"...but rather to '[show] the . . . consequences [of injustice] and throw the challenge to evolve patiently and intelligently a new and better system.'"

the General Convention, chairman of Department of Religious Education for the Bishop and Council, and trustee of the Episcopal Residence (Diocesan House). In 1937 at a special session of Diocesan Convention, he was nominated on the first ballot to become Bishop Coadjutor, but was not elected. He was elected to numerous other offices, however, including:

1938 President of Memphis Ministerial Association

1939 Chairman of Shelby County Inter-Racial Commission

1941-48 on Committee on Diocesan Library, Committee to Raise Funds for the Endowment of the Bishop Gailor Memorial Deanship of the Theological Department of the University of the South

1948 Chairman of Department of Christian Social Service under the Bishop and Council Trustee for Gailor Industrial School

But he didn't do it alone. A charismatic leader, he provided the vision that made his parish wrap its arms around the city, following in their Rector's steps of faith. The Women of the Church worked with women at the penal farm, helping them to find jobs when they were released. They made parish calls, mended toys for needy children, provided lunch for new members, sold calendars to raise money, adopted and outfitted children at the Church Home, served on Better Films Council, the Episcopal Student's Club, the Federated Council of Churches, and the Normal-Buntyn Community Group. The Vestry and the Men's Club provided leadership for the community as well as for the parish. In 1940 Raynor Allen suggested that a committee be organized to create an agency

"No man should regret that he has done good even though others have done evil. . . . What others do is no criterion by which a fine man should judge himself."

to help find work for "persons associated with St. John's, or persons on the social service list of St. John's, or persons who might appeal to the church for help." They balanced the budget despite the Depression, often by contributing whatever was necessary to bridge the gap between receipts and expenses.

In April 1940 a proposal to consolidate Grace Church with St. John's met with very little enthusiasm, and the idea was dropped.

In March 1941 Bishop Maxon sanctioned and authorized the incorporation of St. John's. As the parish grew, the need for a new building took priority. But war delayed the completion of the new church. Plans and fund-raising

accelerated through the early 1940s, with a war bond drive as a major effort. And funds were invested in various savings accounts at various banks, with $10,000 maximum in each, because 1% interest was better than having savings bonds if they were not kept to maturity.

The Rev. Mr. Loaring-Clark turned the first shovelful of dirt for the new building on September 8, 1947. By 1951 the church had grown steadily to 1,125 members, with $71,313 in receipts for the year. On December 30th of that year he baptized his first grandchild, Sarah Elizabeth Jones, daughter of Margaret Loaring-Clark and William Augustus Jones, Jr. (Other children of the Jones' are Martha

Mr. Henry Lancaster, Dr. Jack Henry, The Rev. Mr. Alfred Loaring-Clark, Jack Arthur, The Rev. Mr. Henry Nutt Parsley

Lee Jones Augenstern (Mrs. Fred) whose children are Elise and Julia; Mary Lucile Johnston (Mrs. Andrew) whose children are Neil William and Patricia Austin; and Caroline Ruth Silva (Mrs. Jonathan), expecting their first child in October 1996. Children of Sarah Loaring-Clark and John William Flowers are John William Flowers, Jr. (Jennifer Shipmon) whose children are Ruffin Elizabeth and John William, III; Margaret Lee Ferguson (Mrs. M. Scott) whose children are Michael William and Margaret Loaring; and Martha Austin Hasenmueller (Mrs. Steve) whose children are Austin Lee and William Buckner.)

In a brief article entitled "Myself," Mr. Loaring-Clark wrote that "No man should regret that he has done good even though others have done evil. . . . What others do is no criterion by which a fine man should judge himself."

Alfred Loaring-Clark died suddenly at age 51, just three years after the new church was consecrated.

He had remarked many times that he

The Rev. Mr. Loaring-Clark and the Children's Choir

would like to be buried in the new church. It took work, but his wish was granted by his family, the Bishop, and the health department. Frank Ahlgren helped get permission from the City for the variance from ordinance. Dominican fathers were buried in the crypt of St. Peter's Catholic Church just before Civil War, but the chancel crypt at St. John's was the first of the kind to be used in Memphis since Civil War days. Workers drilled through the 12-inch concrete floor of the chancel, between the two choir stalls. Mr. Henry Lancaster spent the night digging and re-routing wires to prepare the crypt. In modern times such burial has generally been reserved for prelates and kings. The Rev. Mr. Loaring-Clark's burial was just eight days after King George VI was buried in St. George's Chapel at Windsor Castle.

The Order for Burial of the Dead began with a slow processional down the length of the crowded church. Crucifer, torch bearers, acolytes, flag bearers, and clergy, with The Rt.

Rev. Edmund P. Dandridge, D.D., Bishop of the Episcopal Diocese of Tennessee, and The Rt. Rev. Theodore N. Barth, D.D. Bishop Coadjutor officiating. Past senior wardens served as pallbearers below the newly-completed "Christ Triumphant."

Front row, left to right: The Rector, The Rev. Mr. Alfred Loaring-Clark; The Rev. Mr. William A. Jones, Jr.; The Rev. Dr. W.J. Loaring-Clark, Ordination Preacher; The Rev. Mr. Frank McLain; The Rev. Mr. Wallace M. Pennepacker, Associate Rector. Back row: Canon James R. Sharp, Master of Ceremonies; The Rt. Rev. Edmund P. Dandridge, Bishop of Tennessee; The Rt. Rev. Theodore N. Barth, Bishop Coadjutor of Tennessee

After his death, services were held by the Greek Orthodox Church and a mass was celebrated by Father Nenon at St. Anne's Roman Catholic Church. The American Association of Social Workers established a scholarship fund. The Public Affairs Forum gave a memorial to the Episcopal Church fund for educating young ministers.

During the afternoon of the day of Mr. Loaring-Clark's funeral, Dr. Harry W. Ettelson, Rabbi of Temple of Israel Congregation who had shared his dialogues on war during the late 1930s, wrote a poem, which was printed in the March 31, 1952 bulletin.

God Giveth His Beloved Sleep
In Memoriam to my cherished friend Alfred Loaring-Clark

Within the hallowed precincts of this shrine,
Whose finished structure, long ere it was reared,
His mind's eye, with enraptured vision fine,
Beheld in all its richness of design,
As House of Worship, his own Church revered!

In front of altar, where, to rites observant,
He ever ministered, its ordained priest,
His Master's willing and obedient servant,
Giving of self, with equal spirit fervent
To those of high estate, and to the least!

Beneath the chancel, whereon oft he stood,
To intone prayers and to preach the Word,
Stressing the true, the beautiful, the good
With moving eloquence, as well he could,
In terms, whereby minds, hearts and souls were stirred.

'Tis there we've laid most fittingly to rest
The precious mortal frame of him we mourn,
The spot more sacred since of him possessed,
The while his radiant spirit with the Blest
To realms above was lovingly up-borne!

No mist of tears our inner eye must blind,
Nor sound of weeping hush the higher Voice,
'Tis Faith that whispers: "Nobly be resigned;"
'Tis Hope immortal bids us: "Solace find,
He lives, tho dead, and angel hosts rejoice!"

On March 24, 1952, Dr. Harry W. Ettelson presented at the Cross-Cut Club (which The Rev. Mr. Loaring-Clark had helped to found) a tribute to his friend:

> "The sages of the Talmud have a saying: 'Words that come from the heart enter into the heart.'
> . . . Loaring-Clark was one of the moving spirits in organization of the club and served as an early president. Papers he presented showed careful and conscientious preparation, in full respect for the club's high standards, revealed clarity and integrity of his thought and the fine fervor of his spirit. . . . Even dissenting views were presented with over-all geniality and urbanity that took away the sting from the criticism. . . . The prophetic he exemplified by his insistence that Religion must . . . also preach and practice the social gospel in terms of the complex and challenging life of today's world. The pastoral he exemplified by his sympathetic understanding and counseling and his unselfish personal ministrations which reach beyond his own flock to all sorts and conditions of men and women in their everyday human problems and perplexities.
> His character: honor, loyalty, a strong sense of duty, a devotion to truth, a passion for righteousness, a love of peace, a faith in humanity, a kindly interest in people as people and an eager and willing desire to serve them, the saving grace of humor and the spiritual grace of reverent and humble trust in the divine."

The newspapers eulogized The Rev. Mr. Loaring-Clark in long articles about his work, calling him "An Apostle of Peace" who "lived Christ's way as the only way."

An editorial spoke of the man who "built one of the outstanding churches of Memphis." It concluded that "Mr. Loaring-Clark crusaded against evil, particularly persecution in any form and on any scale. His spoken words were eloquent. But his acts were still more eloquent. In a

"An Apostle of Peace" who "lived Christ's way as the only way."

world beset by 'man's inhumanity to man,' Mr. Loaring-Clark so practiced humanity to man that he won a unique place in the hearts of Memphians and the respect of all who knew him."

The memorial fund in his honor has been used specifically for outreach efforts in Memphis. Although income from the fund has fluctuated with economic market conditions, proceeds fund projects deemed worthy but not included in the annual budget of the parish.

He must have felt the crunch of boots stamping across history before Nazi power manifest. And Alfred Loaring-Clark refuted the rhetoric from pulpit and podium throughout the late 1930s.

While thousands cheered the Armistice parade on November 11, 1938, less than 100 others gathered at Idlewild Presbyterian Church to rededicate themselves to the pursuit of peace, led by The Rev. Mr. Loaring-Clark.

He gave the invocation at a brotherhood meeting at The Orpheum Theater, where the keynote speaker, Dr. Alva W. Taylor of Nashville, urged the use of economic boycotts in the fight against Naziism.

*"Tib",
early 1930s*

He misinterpreted the signs throughout the 1930s because they were so foreign to him. Intelligent and intuitive, witty and well-read, he still was not attuned to the winds of change in the world. Truly, they did not reflect his parish, and thus perhaps blindsided him to approaching devastation in the world. But he was very attuned to local events—not as a mere bystander, but as a major player.

When the Democratic Party nominated Franklin Delano Roosevelt, the governor of New York, as its presidential candidate on June 30, 1932, Roosevelt broke tradition and flew out to make an acceptance speech before he was formally notified that the Convention had chosen him. To a country in the economic abyss of the Depression, Roosevelt said, "I pledge you, I pledge myself to a new deal for the American people."

But from December of 1932 to March 1933 the index of industrial production dropped to an all-time low. Concurrently, the banking system crashed. From the beginning of the decade to Roosevelt's inauguration, 5,504 banks closed.

Easter morning at Semmes and Spottswood

The banking crisis, unemployment, and farm relief through curtailed production and the establishment of parity prices set the tone for the new president's first 100 days.

The Great Depression lasted for 42 months in the years of 1929-33. Unemployment mounted to about 15 million in 1933. After only a short recovery, depression struck again for 10 months in 1937-38.

The dollar was devalued by the Gold Reserve Act of January 1934. The Civil Works Emergency Relief Act, Farm Relief Act, Home Owners' Loan Act, Municipal Bankruptcy Act, Corporate Bankruptcy Act, Farm Mortgage Foreclosure Act, Federal Farm Bankruptcy Act, National Labor Relations Act—government attempts to equalize the economy—culminated in the Social Security Act in August 1935. The Fair Labor Standards Act (Wages and Hours Law) passed in 1938 and the Food Stamp Plan in 1939.

St. John's weathered the economic storms by cutting expenses, including the Rector's salary when he offered that in 1932, and by working through each crisis. The budget for 1936 was $7,500, but parishioners did not have the easy income of only a few years previously. The Vestry improvised. When new walks were needed, Dr. Duane Carr offered an old personal debt to be taken out in trade for materials to build walks. The Rector's salary in 1937 was only $3,600; it was increased to $4,000 the following year as the economy eased.

As people across the nation struggled for subsistence, labor versus management, farm worker strife, climatic conditions like the Great Flood of 1937, and other disasters converged toward chaos. That spring, demonstrations

As people across the nation struggled for subsistence, labor versus management, farm worker strife, climatic conditions like the Great Flood of 1937, and other disasters converged toward chaos.

in Chicago for the Steel Workers' union turned into the "Memorial Day Massacre." The Memphis Ministerial Association supported the Mayor's declaration that, "violence will not be tolerated in Memphis" although it is "the right of labor to organize for collective bargaining." The resolutions were presented by The Rev. Mr. Loaring-Clark, after lengthy study by the association's Committee on Social Justice.

That year, he negotiated settlement of a 30-day-old strike between Memphis dress manufacturers and the International Ladies Garment Workers Union, after attempts at settlement had been abandoned. The attorney for the dress company said that, "We would have been out of business had it not been for Mr. Loaring-Clark." But the minister "couldn't see what else they could do" but negotiate a contract.

With all the larger problems came personal disaster. The parish register and all records of St. John's Church were destroyed when the firebug struck the Loaring-Clark home at 371 Patterson during the month of August, while Mr. Loaring-Clark was at Sewanee. No newspaper accounts suggest a political motive, but the firebug struck selected properties before being apprehended.

The battlefront was Europe, but battles were fought in Memphis, too. As war threats intensified, an ecumenical effort to support Jews also accelerated. And The Rev. Mr. Loaring-Clark stood forward as an advocate of peace-making. In a speech in 1938 he said:

"We find ourselves a new parish in a world at enmity within itself. Ours, then, can and must be a parish of reconciliation. We pray for unity and love. No parish can exert such influence in the world until it finds those qualities within itself."

That year, speaking in a Peace Day plea to 400 students gathered at State Teachers College, The Rev. Mr. Loaring-Clark recounted his own experiences as a World War I aviator. He stressed the cost of war in human life and economics, pleading with students to assume leadership in the peace movement. His talk was sponsored by a national college crusade to "Keep the United States Out of War and Promote World Peace."

But he recognized the face of evil in a speech to the Jackson, Tennessee Rotary Club in August 1939, likening Hitler to "the devil, who goeth about as a ravening beast, seeking whom he may destroy. . . . Hitler is a mad man, [and] we cannot remain silent in the presence of this great challenge. . . ."

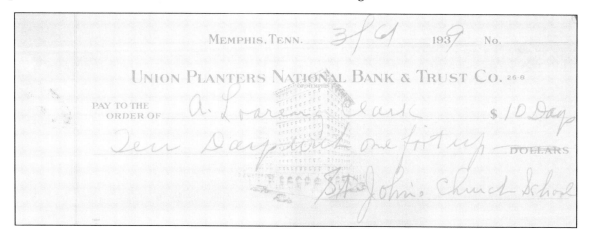

A newspaper article in January 1940 told of a dual discussion, each from the other's point of view, by two of the city's leading clerics. The topic, presented at Temple Men's Club, was "If I were a Jew (Christian)."

Dr. Ettelson said: "If I were a Christian, I would not take my Christianity for granted but I would seek to get at its inner heart and soul. . . ."

Dr. Harry W. Ettelson, Phi Beta Kappa, rabbi of Congregation Children of Israel at Temple Men's Club and The Rev. Mr. Loaring-Clark were the speakers. Dr. Charles E. Diehl, president of Southwestern at Memphis, presided,

leading the forum that followed the talks.

Dr. Ettelson said: "If I were a Christian, I would not take my Christianity for granted but I would seek to get at its inner heart and soul. . . . I would not take His Sermon on the Mount merely as sweet sentiment and glittering generalities. . . . I would not interpret war and tyranny in so-called Christian nations today as representing the failure of Christianity, but . . . interpret it . . . as failure on my part and on the part of other Christians. I would accept it as a challenge to apply Christ's principles to our economic and social system and our national and international relations."

The Rev. Mr. Loaring-Clark said: ". . . I would try to face honestly the world as it is today. . . . I would always remember the name of Abraham for faith. I would know I was a spiritual descendant of Amos, who stood before the world and said God demands righteousness. . . . I would be proud that of the 10 men who have influenced people most, three were Jews—Christ,

Adult choir, 1936

Moses, and Spinoza. But I would not allow my racial prejudices to erect walls and separate me from great men of other races."

Even in November 1941 Alfred Loaring-Clark still did not believe that war with Japan was inevitable. Col. W. J. Bacon, World War I veteran, predicted war before Christmas. Major George Fielding Eliot expressed the opinion that "Japan's . . . air power is almost non-existent." And the Rev. Mr. Loaring-Clark saw events from the perspective of his belief that the Will to Good prevailed in mankind. His writings evidence his staunch faith that the forces for good held the victory.

Despite the economic devastation and impending war, the Rector and St. John's Parish prospered during the decade. From 1932 through 1939 the Parish grew from 175 to 568 communicants. In 1936 buildings were renovated and enlarged to accommodate growth.

Even with expansion the church buildings "bulged at the seams," said the Rector, with the Church School growing faster than building expansion.

Teens of St. John's, 1938

In her oral history interview for St. John's history, Meade Nichol reminisced about the new altar. "Mrs. William Boddie Rogers, Irene Beasley's mother, told me back in 1935 that we needed a new altar. We did, and she said, 'Now, Meade, you collect the money for it and I will pay whatever is lacking.' I collected all I could; ran everybody crazy including myself, and Mrs. Rogers paid the difference. Mr. Osterbrink made it for about $150."

In September 1937 the Rector outlined a three-year expansion program to the Vestry. His goal was to have 500 communicants by the end of the year, to increase the number by 100 each of the next two years, and to launch an ambitious building program during 1940.

Just a year after the church was rebuilt and enlarged, a fire that apparently started in a fuse box destroyed the primary and senior Sunday School departments and a vesting room, ruined the organ, and damaged the roof of the entire building. The fire was reported at almost midnight. Three pumpers and fire truck arrived minutes later, and the prompt response was credited with reducing the damage. There was no fire damage to the nave, but the organ sound box burned. The interior of the church, two pianos, and the Hammond electric organ were badly water damaged. The salvage company placed a heavy tarpaulin over the altar and pews to protect them. The damage was insured, but was estimated at up to $10,000. It was just days before Christmas. Pine boughs covered the charred walls for the annual Christmas Eve Service.

During 1940 there were 27 baptisms, 39 confirmations, 9 burials, 11 weddings, and 36 transfers, to begin 1941 with 619 communicants.

As war accelerated, a newspaper story dated March 7, 1942 quotes The Rev. Mr. Loaring-Clark: "If history is to be understood we must remember that the final meaning of the universe is found in God, not man. His will, not man's, is to be done on earth."

Letters from bishops, clergy, journalists, and friends affirmed the influence of St. John's Parish, led by The Rev. Mr. Loaring-Clark. Edward Meeman, Editor of *Memphis Press-Scimitar* wrote to Mr. Loaring-Clark in January 1942:

". . . I believe very much in the church in general and you in particular. I have just read *The Life of George Herbert* by Izaak Walton. I did not know that the earnestness which ministers such as you show today had a counterpart in the formative ways of your church. . . . The Greatness of England could not be without the greatness of her church. Today, we, England's offspring, must be greater still, if we are to survive at all, and where can we look except to the church . . . ?"

After the Pearl Harbor attack in December 1941, the news grew increasingly grim. The United Nations Declaration was signed by 26 nations, pledging to employ their full military and economic resources against the Axis and promising not to make a separate peace. The battles of Bataan and Corregidor in January began the year 1942 with a litany of foreign names. Macassar Strait. Luftwaffe. The Gilbert Islands. Badoeng Strait. British withdrawal from Rangoon. Fall of Mandalay. The Battle of the Java Sea. Lae and Salamaua in New

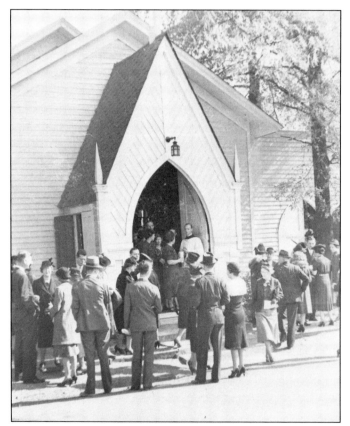

Mr. Loaring-Clark and his congregation

Rally Day Greeting, 1942

Westminster Presbyterian Church
LAMAR AT BELLEVUE
Memphis, Tenn.

SAMUEL E. HOWIE, D. D.
MINISTER

CHRISTMAS 1941

Dear Tib:

Another year has come and gone, almost. It has been a year filled with fears and misgivings. Men of the highest faith and noblest aspirations have found themselves thwarted and frustrated. Many of us have been tempted to give up our faith in our fellows.

I want you to know that through it all, knowing you has been a strong stimulus to my own efforts. You have made it easier to believe in all men. Your friendship has been one of the things that I have cherished most, and you have been a source of inexhaustible inspiration to my own life.

As we face another Year together, we know that it will be a hard year. Men will lose faith in each other and in the noblest dreams they have had. But I shall walk a little steadier, hold my head a little higher and believe a little stronger in the infinite worth of every man because I have come to believe in you. I have resolved, at all costs, to keep my faith in man and in God. Knowing you will make that high resolve easier to keep.

With every sincere good wish, I am

Your friend,

Sam Howie

Guinea. The Battle of the Coral Sea—first naval engagement in history in which all fighting was done by carrier-based planes instead of surface ships engaging enemy ships. Midway. Bremen. The Solomon Islands. Sevastopol.

President Roosevelt asked the nation for a day of prayer on January 2, 1942, and hundreds of Episcopalians flocked to the Cathedral when it opened at 10 a.m.

Just as the growing parish announced plans for a new building, the focus split into concerns for the world and concerns for their church.

Wednesday, March 4, 1942 - Vestry Minutes

Discussion about raising funds to be sent the General Church, to be used for the maintenance, equipment, etc., of Chaplains in the U.S. Armed Forces. Mr. D. T. Kimbrough, Jr. made a motion that Mr. H. P. Jordan be authorized to take such steps as were necessary to raise whatever balance was necessary to complete St. John's quota if not raised on Sunday, March 8, 1942. Seconded by Mr. T. K. Robinson and accepted unanimously by the Vestry.

Once it was impossible for the United States to avoid involvement in the war, "Tib" the pacifist, seemed to see a vision of the Church's war effort as a holy crusade. No one had believed that atrocities against the Jews could quite be true. Newsreels and intelligence reports provided affirmation that the German embrace of Nietsche's "Aryan Super Race" ideology opened the gates of hell. Pacifists of the 1930s prayed for peace—the connotation of that word "pacificist" before antiwar activists changed its meaning decades later. Early on, even before the gruesome news of concentration camps, pacifism ignited into moral outrage that the "war to end all wars" was just a leftover slogan from the first world war. Patriotism crested at the sneak attack on Pearl Harbor, and young and old rushed to enlistment sites.

Ruth Loaring-Clark, the Rector's sister who taught at St. Mary's, was the first Memphis woman to volunteer

"Tib" the pacifist, seemed to see a vision of the Church's war effort as a holy crusade.

for duty with the Red Cross. In March 1942 she reported to headquarters in Washington for the Overseas Recreation Service, to "become part of what is known as a 'Flying Squadron.' "

Wednesday, May 6, 1942 - Vestry Minutes
Suggestion that there be placed in the church yard a table with names and pictures of the boys of St. John's Parish who are serving in the Armed Forces of our Country, so that members of the congregation could write short notes to these boys.

Wednesday, June 3, 1942 - Vestry Minutes
The Clerk of the Vestry, Mr. J. S. Shields, tendered his resignation due to his enlistment in the Armed Forces. Mr. R. M. Hancock elected unanimously to fill his place.

Riding that crest of patriotic fervor, "Tib," World War I aviator, wanted to enlist in the Red Cross Ambulance service, to comfort warriors who wanted to slay the anti-Christ and liberate the good German people duped by rhetoric. A rhetorician himself, he must have known that no war ever started without the words to speak it into existence. And he must have felt compelled to go to war.

The vestry said, "No!"

On April 18, 1942 the War Manpower Commission was established to more effectively use manpower resources. The draft age was lowered to 18; all males up to age 38 were subject to selective service, but clergy were among the few deferment groups.

On July 8, 1942—29 days before the Marines landed at Guadalcanal—Alfred Loaring-Clark petitioned his vestry to let him volunteer with the Red Cross.

Wednesday, July 8, 1942 - Vestry Minutes
Motion and second that all Vestrymen going into the armed services retain their status on the Vestry until their return, at which time they would serve their unexpired term, and that a Vestryman, Pro Tem, be elected to serve in their absence. Unanimously carried.

Dr. Duane Carr brought up the serious transportation problem for choir members trying to get to rehearsals and services.

"The Rev. Mr. Alfred Loaring-Clark then requested the attention of the Vestry to a matter concerning himself and his relation to the Parish. A very full statement was then made as to the length of time in which he had considered the matter and weighed the various details in connection with the request he was about to make of the Vestry. He then stated that he wished to request a leave of absence from the Church to volunteer his services with an ambulance unit abroad. He also requested that the Parish make whatever financial arrangements were possible for the continuance of a part of his salary as he was naturally faced with the continued responsibility of his family as the work into which he wished to volunteer carried no remuneration beyond a bare $15 per month. His reasons for this decision were gone into fully.

Upon the completion of his remarks a very full discussion was entered into with every member

'That the Vestry expresses its complete confidence and love for the Rector and a desire to back him in every way possible.

present taking part. Worded in different ways, it was unanimously expressed, that the sincerity of the Rector's convictions was unquestioned. However, the general fear was expressed by those Vestrymen present that the Parish as a whole would suffer an irretrievable loss by the Rector's absence.

Mr. T. K. Robinson then offered the following motion, which was seconded, and unanimously passed:

'That the Vestry expresses its complete confidence and love for the Rector and a desire to back him in every way possible. That the matter be referred to the Finance Committee with a request that they report back to a called Meeting of the Vestry on Friday night, July 10, 1942, with definite information and recommendations.'"

Friday, July 10, 1942 - Vestry Minutes

"The Rev. Mr. Alfred Loaring-Clark was recognized and read a prepared statement to the Vestry and asked that same be included in the minutes:

'At the meeting of St. John's Vestry Wednesday night, I requested a leave of absence from the Parish to serve with an ambulance unit abroad. I also asked that the Parish make whatever financial arrangements were possible for the continuance of a part of my salary. The request was made after months of thought. It was made honestly. It was made at a time when men are dying by thousands, and we anticipate hundreds of thousands of American men falling on the battlefield.

To this request the Vestry gave both a courteous and commendatory answer. The resolution you passed is spread upon the records of the meeting. Your appointment of the Finance Committee to bring in recommendations regarding financial commitments is also a part of the record. I understand their report is ready at this time.

Before their report is presented, however, I must state that facts unsuspected by me have changed the nature of the situation. I had thought that there would be only one question present in the mind of the Vestry; namely, whether or not such a sacrifice on the part of the Parish would be possible. After talking yesterday and today with five of the Vestrymen, I find my judgment at fault. There is an equally serious question in the minds of the Vestry as to the wisdom of my going abroad to do ambulance work. It would be one thing to be sent abroad as an added financial burden to the Church. It would be impossible for me to accept the support of the Church given reluctantly, without enthusiasm, or against the better judgment of the Vestry. I could go even though I felt an added hardship had been placed on St. John's. I cannot go, accepting support given as a favor rather than a moral demand. My work abroad with wounded and dying men would somehow have to be thought of as the Parish working with and through me.

In time of war none of us can hesitate before added burdens. They must come alike to army, navy, civilian life, church life, and every area of existence. None can escape increased agony of body, mind, or soul. I believe that if the Vestry felt my work abroad were right, the congregation could meet any added burden. But, of course, the church could not and should

'A man is small indeed who cannot meet disappointment and use it for added fineness of mind spirit.'

not accept any added responsibility for an action which they consider unwarranted or unjustified. I could not accept the backing of the Parish given with less than unanimous assent.

Since I believe that my analysis of the thought of the Vestry, as five men have so expressed it, is against my leaving for service with the American Ambulance Service, I therefore withdraw the request made Wednesday night. I have not heard the decision of the finance committee. I have purposely avoided

knowing their recommendation to you. Should they, however, report that my salary will be continued in full, I still cannot go, knowing that the Vestry does not concur wholeheartedly in the wisdom of this act.

I remind you of my final statement last Wednesday evening. I repeat again, that to be denied today the opportunity of serving abroad will in no way impair my serving as Rector of St. John's. A man is small indeed who cannot meet disappointment and use it for added fineness of mind spirit. I have attempted by act, rather than by word alone, to express my sadness and horror of war. I have made the attempt to say to those Christian men from our country that I am willing to stand with them through the ordeal of battle. No one can criticize that desire. I regret it cannot be carried out at this time.'

Mr. E. D. Schumacher moved 'That the statement be received and accepted by the Vestry and that the Committee who were requested to report back to this meeting, their findings, be discharged without their report being made, and further that the Rector be commended for his action and that we assure him of our loyalty and wholehearted cooperation in the future as in the past in his work in the Parish.'

The motion was seconded by Mr. Shubael T. Beasley and unanimously passed."

Wednesday, August 5, 1942 - Vestry Minutes
$101 was given as a memorial to Captain Richard C. McGuire, by his friends and associates, to be used at discretion of Vestry.

D. T. Kimbrough, Jr. and Julian Bondurant resigned. The Vestry agreed that vacancies be filled by elected new Vestrymen to fill balance of term, not as *pro tempore* and that the Vestry be increased as necessary by the reinstatement of any absent Vestrymen who returned prior to the end of his term.

Wednesday, September 9, 1942 - Vestry Minutes
Vestry was asked by The Rev. Mr. Loaring-Clark to write a letter of recommendation to be used along with application for a Commission in the Armed Forces by Barnett Field. T. K. Robinson agreed to write the required letter.

Wednesday, October 7, 1942 - Vestry Minutes
The Rev. Mr. Loaring-Clark announced that Frank McLean, of the Parish, intended to enter Ministry.
Rationing of meat and sugar made it difficult for the Men's Club to serve meals.

The *Stars and Stripes*, established in April as a weekly for the armed forces became a daily by November, and coined the phrase "G.I. Joe." It provided news, but not news of home. The St. John's bulletins began to include more news of people.

Wednesday, November 4, 1942 - Vestry Minutes
Gas rationing makes difficulties for the choir.
Discussion of sending servicemen from the Parish the bulletins and "Forward Day by Day" booklets. Also that a Prayer Book be sent to each one entering and that a medallion cross be sent to each for Christmas.

Sergeant William Graves (Billy) was the first Parishioner lost to the war. Had been Acolyte.

War affected but did not deter the business of the church. On January 6, 1943 the Vestry raised the salary of organist Mrs. Forrest McGinley to $75 per month—an increase of more than 200% in six years—and of church secretary Mrs. Lott to $50 per month.

In February the Ladies Auxiliary sponsored a USO dance, and the Vestry voted $100 of unallocated Christmas Fund money to be used by the Ladies Auxiliary to sponsor monthly USO dances.

At their March meeting, the Vestry decided that, because of rationing, food would no longer be served at Vestry meetings, beginning with the April meeting.

The Ways and Means Committee prepared a brochure to explain the War Savings Stamp Book Plan, while the Women's Auxiliary sponsored a Savings Book.

Patriotism ran high. People supported the war effort in numerous and varied ways. In the April meeting of the Vestry, J. K. Rutland, Jr. brought up the question of the American flag being put back in the church. It was also suggested that a service flag or plaque with the names of the men in the service be placed in the church.

In the May meeting, Mr. Rutland made a motion that a U.S. flag be purchased and that it be carried in the Church procession. E. D. Schumacher and Dr. Duane Carr requested that they be allowed to buy the flag. The Vestry accepted their offer.

The June report to the Vestry proudly announced the largest confirmation class in history—53.

Easter Sunday, 1943

The war effort, with labor shortages, changed employment practices. The Vestry decided in June that Thomas, the janitor, be given two weeks pay for vacation. The organist and secretary were going on vacation, and the Vestry insisted that the Rector also take a vacation, but he said he couldn't.

Tripoli fell to the British Eighth Army in January 1943 and the following month Gen. Eisenhower was appointed commander in chief of all Allied forces in North Africa. Patton's and Montgomery's troops routed Rommel's Afrika Korps and the North African campaign formally ended in May.

March 15, 1944 - Vestry Minutes
> Efforts being made to give men in service who are serving in the Near East an opportunity to visit the Holy Land and Jerusalem by paying their expenses on regularly conducted tours. Good Friday collection to be designated for it.
>
> Voted that $15 be sent to Red Cross.
>
> Kenneth Duncan resigned from Vestry; going into Navy.

May 3, 1944 - Vestry Minutes
> Bulletin should have names, rank, news of parishioners in service.

June 7, 1944 - Vestry Minutes
> Layman's League getting members of all parishes to invite sailors from the Navy base at Millington to spend weekends in their homes.

Despite wage and price controls, national income increased to 2.5 times as much in 1945 as at the beginning of the war. By mid-1944 Mrs. McGinley's salary was raised to $110; Mrs. Lott's to $70.

The parish budget reflected changing economics. The budget for 1945 was:

Altar Expense	$200
Church School	120
Forward Movement	100
Men's Club	150
Music	200
Parish Dinner	150
Young People's Activities	100
Missionary Apportionment	4,153
Diocesan Assessment	538
Sewanee	100
Social Service	420
Rector's Discretionary Fund	100
Army and Navy Commission	500
Church Pension Fund	330
Rent on Rectory	600
Rent on Property Not Owned	60
Building Fund	1,000
Stationery, Supplies and Postage	1,320
Rector's Automobile Expense	300
Salaries	7,950
Repairs and Alterations	750
Every Member Canvass	100

Insurance	200
Convention Expense	100
Operating Expenses	600
Ways and Means Committee	100
Miscellaneous	550
TOTAL	$20,791

oo far to walk from here to you,
So — Cheerio and Toodleoo!

The Raynor-Allen Family

In July 1944 the United Nations Monetary and Financial Conference at Bretton Woods, N.H. was attended by representatives of 44 nations, and established the International Monetary Fund to stabilize national currencies. Throughout that year and the next, conference followed conference: Quebec Conference, 2nd Moscow Conference, Malta Conference, Yalta Conference, United Nations Conference on International Organization, European Advisory Commission, Potsdam Conference, London Conference, Paris Conference. . . . On April 12, 1945 Franklin Delano Roosevelt died of a cerebral hemorrhage. His death was called "a casualty of war, who died in action, defending the rights of man."

The six months battle over the Philippines (June 19 to December 15, 1944) ended in a decisive defeat of the enemy. Gen. MacArthur's forces, invading in the central Philippines, began the drive to retake the islands. But the devastation was astronomical in mid-1940s dollars.

June 6, 1945 - Vestry Minutes

Church Reconstruction Program in Philippines to cost $3.5 million; St. John's assessed for $3,200 contribution.

V-E Day celebrated the formal end of the war in Europe, followed by V-J Day, but the flock was still scattered.

Dear Communicants in the Armed Forces:

Jean Hazlehurst, home from Sweet Briar and her usual enthusiastic self, said to the Rector last week, "Since there's no bulletin for two months, let's send some word from the Parish to our men and women with the Armed Forces." It's a grand idea and this letter comes to you in lieu of our bulletin. We assure you that you are not forgotten.

A few hours ago, news was released that the Japanese war is successfully concluded. Of course, we are more grateful than words can express, and will have prayers of thanksgiving tomorrow and on Sunday morning. Memphis is taking the news quietly, though Joe Boyle says we may make all the noise we want for 24 hours. We suspect the end of hostilities will be received with gratitude and prayerful thanksgiving.

Here are a few items about St. John's. The parish is still financially strong, the budget balanced, and no indebtedness. Ted Fox, as chairman of finances, and Jim Taylor, treasurer, are doing a bang-up job with finances. We might add that perhaps the congregation deserves some credit for giving the money enthusiastically and regularly.

Plans for the new church are going on apace. Within the week we will have settled definitely the architectural arrangements of our buildings. As you know, the general style is Williamsburg Colonial architecture, and when completed, our church and parish buildings will be very lovely. If priorities are released, we should begin construction in a few months.

The Church School is flourishing, crowded to capacity, and with a fine faculty for this fall. Our enrollment is still about 300, which is our maximum capacity.

Some 20 odd youngsters from St. John's went to Camp Gailor-Maxon, had a grand time, and walked off with a lot of honors. Young Charles D. Richardson was elected Crusader Spirit Boy, while Teddy Fox was chosen as Camp Spirit Boy. Teddy followed the trail blazed by both his other brothers who, in their day, won the same honors. Virginia Jones and Sarah Loaring-Clark were elected to the Honor Ring.

Is it disloyal to you people who are fighting through the blood, sweat, and tears of the battlefronts to tell you that the Rector and Sam Carey, Senior Warden, stole away last week for a fishing trip down the White River? It's a beautiful, peaceful stream, flowing through the mountains, though we gave the bass no peace and really had fine luck. The Senior Warden, whom most of you know to be a fine Christian gentleman, lived up to his high ecclesiastical honor even in his sleep at night. The guide and the Rector were startled at 3am by a burst of oratory by the sleeping Sam Carey who ended by saying, "All I want to do is to be fair." From that time on every fish that got away was the result of Sam's trying to be fair.

Probably you are most interested in hearing something of your friends from St. John's who are scattered to the four corners of the earth, so here goes.

Shubael Beasley, after two and a half years in the Pacific with the Navy, is now training in the U.S. for his commission.

Cress Fox, who flew for two years with the Navy in the Pacific, came home last month and is now a Naval attache in South America.

Johnny Bishop has been to Europe with the Army and is now stationed in Florida.

The Sutton brothers are both in the Air Corps. Willis made a grand record flying the Hump for 24 months, and is now instructing in this country. Some two months ago he married a very lovely girl in St. John's. Brother Albert Sutton went through the Normandy invasion and at present is in Germany.

John Palmer reports himself well and has never had to leave this country.

Tommy Lincoln has had a couple of Air Craft (sic) carriers shot out from under him in the Pacific. He came through practically unhurt until stationed in this country: he fell off a watch tower and broke a leg.

Mike Sinclair is doing valiant service with the Paymaster's Corps in England.

Wallace Locke has been out in the Pacific with the Navy for several years.

Richard Mueller is flying Helldivers for the Navy, but so far has had no overseas service.

Lee Cooper is flying for the Navy and is stationed in Brunswick, Maine.

Barney Fields has been in England with the Air Corps for two and a half years, and we judge from his letters is about to come home.

Young Ben Dyer, who has been with the Navy since Pearl Harbor and in a lot of heavy fighting, came home last week and took for himself a swell wife.

George Stone has been stationed with the Army for two years.

Lowell Sturup has seen most of the heavy fighting in Europe since D-Day, and at last report has not received so much as a scratch.

Clarke Reynolds is stationed with the Army in Ft. Knox, Kentucky.

Robert Palmer has been overseas for sometime with the 16th Armored Division, and has seen quite heavy fighting.

Ruth Loaring-Clark, who was with the first Red Cross Unit to go into Australia, came home last Christmas looking fit, and is now stationed just outside Manila.

Bayard Boyle has been on Gen. Lear's staff overseas for the last 18 months and is now ready to receive his discharge.

Frank White, who went to the Pacific with one of the first Marine outfits, and has been through four major landings, including Iwo Jima, is still in the Pacific and complains lustily (and justly) about not getting home.

Russ Pritchard, who was sunk in the Mediterranean, came home several months ago and is now back in the Pacific theater with the Navy.

Earl Nichols had the same experience of being sunk in the North Atlantic but is now stationed in England.

Teddy Kimbrough, who commanded LST's from the Aleutians to Saipan, and all intermediate points, is now stationed in a subdued port in Virginia and laments vociferously that the Navy is turning him every way but loose.

Minor Atkinson, with the Air Corps, has been in North Africa, Sicily, Italy, and now in France. He hopes to be home by Christmas.

James Shields, who we believe has been a super duper sleuth with the Intelligence Department, never reveals his present whereabouts but we know he has been at various points in the Pacific.

Fred Boehme, who has been stationed in England for the past two years, is now reported on his way home and headed for discharge.

Hugh Thompson is somewhere in the S. Pacific helping Admiral Halsey.

Henry Lancaster, who entered the Army the first few weeks of war, has never been home, being shuttled from island to island and is now in or near Manila.

Ralph Lewis, Gunner on a B-24, has been through Italy and is now stationed in Texas.

Frederick Thirkield is stationed down in Florida after duty in European waters.

Everett Cook, who won fame with Gen. Spatz, is discharged and back with his cotton business in Memphis.

Eugene Caruthers has been stationed in this country with the Army for two years and is now stationed in Texas.

Charles Beacham has been with the Signal Corps in the Pacific for some 18 months and is still out in that theater.

Richard Reynolds, who won fame in St. John's by marrying Ann Tuthill, spent two years with the Navy in the Pacific and is now stationed outside of Boston. They are to be congratulated on having a bouncing boy.

Tommy Price is still somewhere in Germany with the Army.

Turner Morehead is back on furlough after flying Helldivers with the Navy all over the Pacific.

David Fox, who spent two years flying Thunderbolts in England and France, came home last week weighing 198 pounds and having the distinction of shooting down the first German jet propelled plane.

Frances Shumacher, Sgt. in the WACS, has been doing valiant recruiting service in this country.

Brooks Walker has been with the Navy in the Pacific for over two years and came home resplendent with citations.

Tunkie Saunders has been stationed the past year with the Army in Washington.

Bobbie Robinson came home from England, France, and Germany last month and is just before taking himself a wife.

Horace Twiford has been overseas for 18 months and at last report was stationed in Northern France.

William Highberger has been doing camouflage and engineering work with the Army, and is now stationed in Virginia.

Walter Hughes has been flying pursuit planes in France and is still overseas.

Frank McLain, postulant, after being sent to 3 universities by the Army, was recently transferred to the Medical Corps and expects to be sent soon to the Pacific.

John Boyd, tall and popular B-24 pilot, got shot at considerably in Italy and is now flying 29's and ready to go to the Pacific.

Billy Graham likewise flew in Italy with distinction and is now doing transition in the U.S.

John Dorsey is in the Army, stationed somewhere out in the far Pacific theater.

Thomas Wright was stationed by the Navy in this country for about a year, but is now somewhere in the Pacific.

John Ragland was pushed about from camp to camp in this country until finally they sent him to some island in the Pacific where he is now stationed.

Peggy Little, signal officer deluxe, is stationed in the Marines in North Carolina.

William Marsh is still stationed at Bowdin College in Maine.

Ray Bauman fortunately has been stationed in Memphis at the Ferry Command ever since he enlisted.

Caleb Dorsey is with the Air Corps in Galveston, Texas.

Jack Arthur has been wailing for two years asking to be transferred from Ft. Monroe, Va. but is still there.

Felder Morehead has been starring as a V-12 student at Yale, and it now looks as though he will finish the war with his Engineering Degree.

Jane Chilton Phillips was stationed in Washington for a year and is now stationed in Memphis.

Ernest Shumacher, erstwhile vestryman, is gunner now on a transport and has been plowing the Pacific for some 20 months.

Louis Berry has been stationed with the Army in England for about 18 months.

Willard Ward has been a purchasing agent in the Navy for the past 2 years and stationed at Lexington, Ky.

Leo Fristrom, originally stationed by the Coast Guard in Florida, was sent to Europe some six months ago.

Jack Hall, paratrooper, has been jumping all over Europe and is expected to jump home next month.

Jane Sutton covered herself with glory as an Army Nurse in Nashville and is now stationed at Plattsburgh.

Ronald Hopton, aboard a destroyer for 18 months, has been home once and is now cruising the Pacific.

Earl Payne has been in Europe for some 12 months but we don't know where he is now stationed.

Emmett Hall is still training as a flyer with the Navy.

John Stout has been doing a V-5 course at Sewanee but the Navy has sent him recently to Louisiana for flight training.

Spurgeon Neal (who you know married Alice Torti) is with the Army somewhere in Europe.

Thomas Livingston was sent by the Navy two years ago to the Pacific and is still out there.

Charles Seay returned yesterday from 12 months in the Pacific with the Navy. He hopes for a discharge soon.

Robert Carl Clarke did a grand job with the Army in France, was considerably shot up, and is now hospitalized in Nashville.

Denleigh Clarke is doing a V-12 course for the Navy at Georgia Tech. We have him home occasionally.

Horace White is home after a frightful but interesting experience in Holland. His P51 was shot down and he fortunately landed in Holland where he spent three months with the Dutch underground. The Gestapo finally caught him and he was placed first in a concentration camp, then in a prisoner of war camp. He is back now, looking none too worn from his experience.

Schuyler Williams is off with the Navy in the Pacific.

Fred Muller is stationed with the Naval Engineers in Washington.

Young George (Bud) Howell is plowing back and forth in the North Atlantic with the Navy.

Percy and Russell Wood are with the Navy and Army respectively, both stationed in this country.

Sidney Davis has affected landings on several Pacific islands where he has been for 18 months.

Justin Davis has been cruising the Pacific with the Navy for some 12 months, but last Sunday was in church. His brother Carl is a Ranger somewhere in Europe.

Archie MacLaren is with the Artillery in Louisiana, never having left this country.

John Franklin heaves his 185 pounds into the ball turret of a B-17. He was at home two weeks ago on furlough.

Henry Walker has been out in the Pacific with the Navy for some six months.

Ward Treverton, who made many friends during his brief sojourn in Memphis, has been in England and Europe for many months.

Tommy Dodson, who had his feet frozen in Europe and convalesced in Paris, came home a month ago bright and chipper. He probably leaves for new assignment in a few days.

Sam Hitt (who married Harriet Thompson) has been sent by the Navy to the Pacific.

Ken Duncan, erstwhile vestryman, is still held by the Navy at Lakehurst.

Irrepressible Rogers Beasley is still bubbling over, albeit in the Philippines. His bright, radiant letters assure us the Army hasn't changed him.

Stuart Robbins has been in Europe for lo these 16 months.

Lafayette Woolwine (Bill to you) is stationed by the Army in Central America.

Eddy Atkinson is cruising the high seas in an LSM.

Milton Miller has been in Europe for some 18 months.

Jim McDonnell is doing a V-12 course at Sewanee.

Carroll Cooper is about ready to complete his flying with the Navy.

Dick Walker, who has done a swell job with Ordnance, is about to wind up and come home.

Robert Scrivener is somewhere is the vast Pacific with the Navy.

Glenn Allen had his picture spread all over the Press Scimitar last week. He did extraordinary work with the medics in France and picked up several medals.

William Walker followed his brother into the Navy and is still stationed in the U.S.

Young Bobby Morrow is with the Navy and at last report was still in California.

Dick Leatherman is doing a V-12 course down at Millsaps College.

Jerome York, who entered the Army a few years ago as a Lt., was in church last Sunday wearing silver leaves. He has made most of the way stations in the Pacific, and looks grand after his experience.

Larry McSpadden is doing a V-12 course at Sewanee.

Hunter Shawhan (the original G-I Joe) is doing an ASTP course at Blacksburg, Va.

Sammy Cone, who entered the Navy a few weeks ago, has finished boot and is at Gulfport, Miss.

Tim Treadwell has had rare experiences flying cub planes in France with the Army. He came home last week.

James Harrison has done swell work with the Infantry in France and Belgium.

Winston Cheairs, whose eye sight prevented him from joining the Armed Forces, went with the American Field Service to Burma. At last reports he was sweating it out in the jungles.

Mrs. Joe Mulherin (Mary Jo Tate) joined the Red Cross since her husband is in India and is doing grand recreational work in a hospital in Florida.

Milton Adams was commissioned three months ago by the Navy and is now doing plastic surgery in the Naval Hospital in Oakland, Calif.

Burnet Tuthill of Southwestern and Symphony fame was selected to set up music schools for American troops in England and France. For some weeks now he has been commuting between London and Paris.

J. E. Strassner is in boot camp at Great Lakes.

Earl King is doing a V-12 course at Georgia Tech.

Howard Dyer is at Camp Wheeler, Ga. toughing it out with the Infantry.

Last to leave St. John's is Major Vansant, who with his wife was confirmed in our last class. He is on his way to the Pacific.

Since we began this bulletin, there is every indication that the war is being concluded. Please believe that we rejoice as much as you do that you will soon be home. Your parish, which has tried to maintain the same high standards during the war, is waiting eagerly to give you a welcome home.

Alfred Loaring-Clark
Jean Hazlehurst, Amanuensis

After victory was won, St. John's created a silver memorial chalice to commemorate the six young parishioners sacrificed to the war. Six precious stones of different colors were inset into the stem. The names, dates, and branches of service were engraved on the inside of the Chalice base: William Preston Graves, Air Corps, 1920-1942, ruby; Lawrence McCormick, Jr., Air Corps, 1921-1943, amethyst; John Manche Bennett, Infantry, 1922-1944, emerald; William Hudson Byrd, Air Corps, 1911-1944, sapphire; Fred Cook Beacham, Infantry, 1919-1945, topaz; Thomas Gregory Dabney, Navy, 1913-1945, rose zircon. The Rector surely was the author of the statement that "It was thought fitting that this sacred vessel commemorate those whose life blood was given for freedom and brotherhood as was their Master's."

The first stone for the chalice—the single amythest on a cross in the base—was given by The Crusaders in memory of 15-year-old Louie Ensinger Burt, killed in a freak auto accident in 1941.

Despite the many war deprivations, the faithful parishioners had steadily worked toward the new building needed to accommodate the growing church. Throughout the dark early years of the decade they held forth hope for materials and resources becoming available after the war. Planning accelerated after the victory.

November 7, 1945 - Vestry Minutes
Lucian Dent (architect) is to be thanked for designing a new cover for bulletin.

December 5, 1945 - Vestry Minutes
Lucian Dent is to be asked to design a stand for the new memorials book.

W. L. Nichol, former senior warden and chairman of the Building Committee reported estimated costs for new building, based on blueprints, at $400,000+.

Mr. Taylor, treasurer, recommended and the Vestry voted to give The Rev. Mr. Loaring-Clark $1,000 (from the $2,800 on hand) since he was "sure the Rector's expenses were large and that his salary was not all that it should be, and of his great interest and untiring efforts in discharging successfully the duties of his office."

Morris Beutel of S&W Construction gave the estimate (free) for construction of the new building. Lucian Dent was paid $1,500 for services to date as architect.

January 1946 - Annual Meeting
$78,351.12 in cash & pledges for the new building. The building size was changed to seat 500, not 648. It was recommend that the church hire an associate rector, a full-time secretary, and a director for the Church School.

February 6, 1946 - Vestry Minutes
W. L. Nichol, Chairman, H. W. Lancaster, Herbert Jordan, and D. T. Kimbrough were nominated as permanent building committee and elected by acclamation.

It was agreed that the bulletins should be mailed second class.

The Rev. Mr. Loaring-Clark was given a raise of $100 per month.

April 3, 1946 - Vestry Minutes
It was recommended that St. John's acquire a manse for the Rector's family.

May 8, 1946 - Vestry Minutes
Mr. Shubael T. Beasley had talked with W. M. Bell, owner of the residence in which the Loaring-Clarks lived (2946 Southern Avenue), and had agreed to buy it for $8,500, to be paid $1,000 in cash and $73.99 per

month, tax free. Needed repairs were estimated at $3,745.

June 3, 1946 - Vestry Minutes
Despite the end of rationing, choir transportation was still a problem.

Mrs. Lott resigned; Mrs. Edward T. Reece, wife of a vestryman, would be the new full-time secretary.

If symbols for the 1940s were catalogued, fire would surely be high on the list. From newsreels at the movies of bombed cities burning to the Holocaust horrors to renewed popularity of *Keep the Home Fires Burning* to the sentimental *I Don't Want to Set the World on Fire (I Just Want to Start a Flame in Your Heart)*, this primal symbol of both destruction and warmth was prominent throughout the decade.

St. John's experienced the destructive force of fire numerous times in its history. In March 1941 the Property Committee was directed by the Vestry to have repairs made to a window damaged by fire. And just when destruction seemed past and life renewed, fire struck the newly acquired Rectory. The loss, covered by insurance but still loss, was $5,451, reported at the Annual Meeting on January 15, 1947.

Wednesday, March 5, 1947 - Vestry Minutes

The Rev. Mr. Henry Nutt Parsley, the new assistant Rector, was warmly welcomed.

Mrs. Lott was presented with a gold cross in recognition of her 10 years of service.

A motion was made and seconded to authorize Mr. Jordan, Finance Committee Chairman, to have another telephone line and extension installed at a cost of $8.79 per month.

Mr. Lancaster, Property Chairman, requested authorization to spend up to $250 for changes in the

If symbols for the 1940s were catalogued, fire would surely be high on the list.

Rector's offices for additional office space for Mr. Parsley. Motion made and seconded, carried.

Mr. Reece, Music Committee Chairman, reported that Mr. L. Fergus O'Connor was expected around the first part of May, and that cost of his passage would be refunded to him upon his arrival.

Mr. Loaring-Clark stated that he had received a letter from Miss Jean Hazlehurst advising that she was looking forward to assuming her duties as Director of Religious Education sometime around the first of July.

ST. JOHN'S
EPISCOPAL CHURCH

SEMMES AVENUE AT SPOTTSWOOD

MEMPHIS, TENN.

THE PARISH PROGRAM
EXPRESSED IN DOLLARS AT
WORK FOR THE KINGDOM

1945

The first associate rector was a young "Tarheel" named Henry Nutt Parsley. Born in Wilmington, North Carolina, he graduated from University of North Carolina at Chapel Hill and took his B.D. degree at Virginia Theological Seminary. After graduation there he served from 1937-39 as assistant curate at Grace Church in Amherst, Massachusetts and religious education assistant at Amherst College. His experience in working with students at Duke especially pleased the Vestry in considering him for the very active and growing group of young parishioners at St. John's.

Wednesday, April 9, 1947 - Vestry Minutes

The Rector stated that Mr. William Nichol had installed, without cost to the church, a prie-dieu. Motion was duly made, seconded, and carried, that the Clerk of the Vestry write a letter of appreciation to Mr. Nichol.

Shortly after the new organist, Fergus O'Connor, arrived in early May, he became ill and was hospitalized. The expenses amounted to between $100 and $150. But the existing post-war prohibition against taking more than a nominal sum out of England meant that Mr. O'Connor did not have the required amount. The Vestry voted that the hospital expenses be paid out of the emergency fund and that Mr. O'Connor "be requested not to make reimbursement."

Wednesday, June 4, 1947 - Vestry Minutes

$600 due the architects as further payment for work on new buildings.

Wednesday, July 30, 1947 - Vestry Minutes

Vestry approved letting a contract for S&W Construction Company to construct the foundations of the church building and the basement of the church school section, for a sum not to exceed $38,000 plus installation costs for mechanical equipment. Upon completion of the foundations, the company would enter into a contract on a cost plus basis for the completion of the church at a cost of $144,280, subject to a credit of $38,000 expended for the foundations.

Mr. Lancaster was made permanent chairman of the Building Committee, replacing Mr. Nichol, who had resigned.

The Rector announced that the dedication of the new lot and the ceremony of breaking ground for construction of the new church would be Tuesday, September 9 at 4:30 p.m.

At the end of July Mrs. Clarence Saunders, President of the Woman's Auxiliary, outlined to the Vestry the

The Rector announced that the dedication of the new lot and the ceremony of breaking ground for construction of the new church would be Tuesday, September 9 at 4:30 p.m.

imperative need for immediate repairs to the present kitchen, stating that she had obtained an estimate for the necessary work in the amount of $512.35, of which the

Woman's Auxiliary could pay $100. She requested that the Vestry authorize expenditure of the balance. After discussion, the Vestry approved spending $350.

However, at the next meeting the Treasurer advised the Vestry that there was a small overdraft in connection with repairs to the kitchen; the actual repair bill amounted to $432.25. Payment was approved and ratified, and the Clerk of the Vestry was authorized to write a letter to thank Mrs. Saunders for her splendid services.

Wednesday, October 8, 1947 - Vestry Minutes
Bishop Dandridge, after being advised of problems in connection with the construction program, requested that money for the Presiding Bishop's Fund go to apportionment fund, and some plate offering during the year be given to the Presiding Bishop's fund. $5,658 was reapportioned.
Mr. Parsley to be married.

Wednesday, February 4, 1948 - Vestry Minutes
Increased allocation for operation of the Rector's automobiles in the amount of $25 each month.
$1,200 set aside for emergency fund.

Wednesday, May 12, 1948 - Vestry Minutes
Mrs. Reece resigned as secretary; Mrs. Rutland to be employed as of September 1, 1948. Motion passed to employ another employee in office, whose primary duties it would be to aid the Sunday School Superintendent until such time as a full director could be employed.

That June, the Vestry "noted with alarm that the accumulated expense for stationery, supplies, and postage totalled a figure of within $350 of the annual budget for these supplies, and the motion passed unanimously to take up the matter with the Rector on his return." At the July meeting, after discussion with Mr. Loaring-Clark, all agreed that such expenses were due to joyful growth of the parish and the vestry agreed to increase the budget.

Wednesday, October 6, 1948 - Vestry Minutes
Property Committee chairman, Mr. Hopton, reported that in his opinion the Church needs a handyman to fix minor items.

A newspaper for the Church was proposed, to keep Parishioners knowledgeable and involved with activities.

Wednesday, January 5, 1949 - Vestry minutes

Mr. Julian Bondurant, Finance Committee Chairman, reported that as a result of the Every-Member Canvass, pledges totalling $37,740.15 were received. This was some $1,500 more than was anticipated and included more than 100 new pledges. Pledges to the Building Fund totalled $32,906.50.

St. John's was in a growth period, but did not take for granted that it would continue without effort. In February, the Executive Committee was asked to look at activities of other parishes and recommend to the Vestry what would be worthwhile for St. John's.

St. John's Bulletin - September 25, 1949

SO YOU DON'T WANT JAPAN?

For part of the coming year, the whole Woman's Auxiliary of the Episcopal Church will study Japan—its history, contemporary problems and particularly the work of our church there . . .

Well, we're either going to live happily with the Japanese or we are going to fight them. There are some sixty-five millions of Japanese people who inhabit this same planet, have much the same desires, need the same food and wish the same security as we. We had best learn to understand them and they to understand us.

The parents of many a fine lad are distressed that our grandfathers did so little to understand and form strong ties of affection with the Japanese. I hope our grandchildren won't have to look back at us with the same regret.

Isn't the major tragedy of Russia today that they have lowered an Iron Curtain between themselves and us and refuse to "study" us or to have anything to do with us? How tragic we were to ape Russia in our attitude toward Japan!

– A.L-C.

Wednesday, January 12, 1950 - Annual Meeting

The Rev. Mr. Loaring-Clark reported that the present number of communicants was 1,026. Income for 1949 was $41,760.96.

"Entire membership rose in tribute to the fine work done by our Rector, as well as our love for him personally . . ."

Although begun in chaos, the decade ended in a glorious growth period for St. John's.

Children of St. Peter's Church, Yamagata, Japan, wearing and holding gifts sent to them by children of St. John's, Memphis. The gifts were made at a Lenten work party under the direction of Mrs. Charles King.

New Building

In 1922, when Mrs. Palmer Farnsworth asked Mrs. Walter Lott (Gertrude) to come to St. John's and sing in the choir, the small church building accommodated the small congregation. But the parish grew rapidly after The Rev. Mr. Loaring-Clark became Rector in 1928. The Vestry patched and pieced the property together as walls bulged with increasing attendance. Then the Great Depression thwarted expansion plans.

Damage from the firebug's arson at the rectory resulted in an expansion of the church staff. Destruction of early records was nearly total when the arsonist struck the library at the rectory, but the communicant list was salvaged. However, it was scorched so badly that a new list was required. The Rector decided that he must have

"...for the first time in its history St. John's doesn't owe a dime..."

some help. The Parish felt that they could not pay a secretary, so Mr. Loaring-Clark hired Mrs. Lott as the first Parish secretary, paying her from his own salary.

Throughout the 1930s the Parish grew. Walls were knocked out, expansion of any possibility was considered, and the church continued to prosper.

Finally, at the Annual Meeting in 1939, Mr. J. K. Rutland, Jr., Clerk of the Vestry, reported that "for the first

time in its history St. John's doesn't owe a dime," and that the year started off with $130 on hand. The balanced budget was about $13,000 annually, the parish was debt-free, and there were more than 600 communicants.

Vestry minutes for September 3, 1941 first mention plans for a new church. The Vestry agreed to appoint a committee to discuss plans and to secure a working sketch for a new building.

From discussion recorded in Vestry minutes, it must have been difficult for the conscientious stewards of church funds to approve expenditure for a building—no matter how dearly needed—until funds were raised. Mrs. Lott related in her reminiscences that Mr. E. D. Schumacher came into the office one morning and told Mr. Loaring-Clark that he thought it could be done. He raised $77,000 in contributions. Then the question arose:

Mr. E.D. Schumacher

which should be built first—the church, or the church school building?

The new building was announced at the Annual Meeting on January 19, 1942, and projected to have a seating capacity of 800. It would be built at Central and Greer. The new lot was 165 feet on Central Avenue, 315 feet on Greer, and 230 feet on Overland, given by Mr. and Mrs. James Frederick Smith.

From the chatty, small-town tone of the newspaper article about the event, it's evident that the Annual Meeting was, despite the prolonged war, a time of joy and celebration:

> Colossal chef hats were the thing on Wednesday night worn, as they were, by the vestrymen presiding at the buffet table at the annual parish dinner at St. John's Episcopal Church . . . saw Charlie Richardson and Dr. Burnet Tuthill doing a bang-up job on two big turkeys . . . Beth and Herbert Jordan glad to hear from Raynor Allen that young Ann Allen is home from the hospital after an operation . . . Jessica Barton chatting over a cup of coffee with the Bill Terrys . . . Mary and Tom Robinson in a group with Libba and Sam Carey . . . Louise Carr, picture pretty in a pastel ensemble, with husband, Dr. Duane, talking to Mrs. C. N. Burch, whose black hat was flower-fancy with a pair of turquoise blossoms . . . Irene Beasley, in a new-for-Spring chapeau of navy blue with pink roses, and husband, Shubael, in a foursome with Tschudy and Dr. Jack Henry . . . and Clara and The Rev. Alfred Loaring-Clark overjoyed, as were all those present, with the news that

the thousands of dollars, set as a goal by the Building Committee, have been promised . . . the new and long-needed church will be under construction just as soon as war-time restrictions permit . . . only necessary building should be thought of in times such as these, but St. John's has literally worn out and out-grown its present structures . . .

They placed the limit of cost at $30,000, and voted to authorize the appointment of Lucian M. Dent as architect. But they underestimated escalating costs.

The first blueprint, showing a floor plan and some elevations of the proposed new building designed in Gothic architecture, was prepared by Dent, and the cost was estimated at $300,000. The Vestry had anticipated the cost to be about $65,000.

When the first conversations concerning the planning and building of St. John's took place, the Rector, The Rev. Mr. Alfred Loaring-Clark, wanted a Gothic church. The architect, Mr. Lucian Minor Dent, said that he wanted something that would express America. He had

Mr. Lucian M. Dent

worked on the restoration of Williamsburg, Virginia, and was very enthusiastic about Georgian architecture. So he persuaded Mr. Loaring-Clark and the building committee to choose the Georgian style.

Despite differences, the design was reminiscent of historic Bruton Parish Church in Williamsburg, designed by famous English eccliastical architect, Sir Christopher Wren.

Many of you may note a similarity between St. John's and Bruton Parish Church. True, Bruton Parish Church served as an inspiration. It is Georgian, but there the similarity ends. To begin with, St. John's is more than twice as large as Bruton Parish, which seats approximately 250 people, while St. John's seats over 500. The St. John's tower room and spire are entirely different from Bruton Parish, and the interiors of the two churches are entirely different. The plan of St. John's is the Basilican plan.

- Lucian Minor Dent

The buildings of the new church complex were completed in stages, with financing carefully pacing construction. The building fund grew with pledges and gifts ranging from fifty cents of little Diana Carr's allowance—earned from Saturday chores—to the perennial three largest gifts of $5,000 from Mr. Fred Smith, $3,000 from Mr. Arthur Fulmer, and $2,000 from Anonymous.

In his report to the Parish on January 13, 1943, The Rev. Mr. Loaring-Clark wrote about "the necessity of more space both in the church and in the church buildings . . .

[since] sometimes people must stand in the back of the church on Sundays, until the children leave. Others must sit in chairs in the aisles, others sometimes in pews behind the choir. . . . With no sub-flooring in parts of the

. . .sometimes people must stand in the back of the church on Sundays, until the children leave. Others must sit in chairs in the aisles, others sometimes in pews behind the choir. . . .

church, the building is cold [but] there are worse things than having a crowded church improperly heated. . . . Better a crowded church with people struggling to find seats, than one where one sits alone and wonders where the other Communicants can be."

The ground-breaking ceremony in September 1947 was both solemn and festive. At 4:30 in the afternoon, parishioners gathered on the vacant lot to consecrate the

From A Parable of a Parish booklet

Boys' Choir Caroling, 1948

new site. The newly-formed Boy's Choir, organized by Fergus O'Connor, sang in public for the first time. A visitor to the ceremony was the first lay president of the Federal Council of Churches of Christ, who was in Memphis for a speaking engagement.

Wednesday, December 3, 1947 - Vestry Minutes
> Mr. H. W. Lancaster, property committee chairman, stated that it was anticipated that the present construction phase of the new church would be completed some time next week.
> Mr. D. T. Kimbrough, member of the Building

Erecting the facade

Committee, stated that, by making a few minor changes, the estimated cost of the new building could be reduced by the sum of about $40,000. The building committee received unanimous authorization to place an order for the purchase of necessary steel for the construction of the building.

Mr. H. P. Jordan stated that he had made inquiries concerning the possibility of obtaining a loan, if, in the judgment of the Vestry, it became necessary and that he had been assured by a responsible party that a loan of up to $30,000-$35,000 could be obtained at a rate of 4% interest, payable over a period of years.

Wednesday, January 14, 1948 - Annual Meeting

Mr. Jordan, Finance Committee Chairman, reported that all basic obligations had been met and that the sum of $62,000 had been raised for the building fund campaign; that the Building Committee had revised its plans and that the funds on hand would fall about $11,000 short of being sufficient to complete the contemplated plans for the first stage; that it was his conviction that this additional amount could be raised by autumn, and that in any event, it was a manageable deficit.

Wednesday, January 7, 1948 - Vestry Minutes

Mr. Lancaster, chairman, reported that an order for the necessary steel had been placed with Pidgeon-Thomas Iron Co. and that delivery was expected around the first of April. After shortages for the whole decade, it was good news.

Wednesday, October 6, 1948 - Vestry Minutes

Mr. Alfred B. Pittman reported that he and Mr. Loaring-Clark had a conference with Mr. Dent concerning liability of the church for architect's fees in connection with church furnishings. Mr. Dent stated that, in his opinion, he was entitled to an architect's commission on the cost of any parts or furnishings for the interior of the church which were included in the drawings and specifications.

However, he also stated that he would waive any claim for commissions that might otherwise be due in connection with the installation of the pews, and further stated that any member of the church or its representative could feel free to call upon him at any time for advice concerning furnishings or interior parts of the church without expectation of paying any architect's fee therefor (stet) unless advised in advance that a charge would be made for such advice or service. It was the consensus that a letter be written by the Clerk to the firm of Dent and Aydelott, expressing appreciation for their kindness, and outlining the understanding.

Wednesday, October 6, 1948 - Vestry Minutes

Mr. Gregg reported that early delivery of new pews for the future St. John's was apparently impossible and it was decided that his committee would proceed to secure these pews as fast as possible, but that temporary arrangement to use the present pews would be made, supplemented by chairs.

Delay in completion of the roofing contract held up final completion of church building until after January 1. In March 1949 a contract was let for $43,000 to construct space for church offices, church school, the nursery, vestry, choir, and coffee hour. The new location at the corner of Central and Greer needed landscaping. The Vestry voted that it should not exceed $1,000.

January 30th was the coldest, snowiest day of that winter. The air was too cold for the mortar to stick when The Rev. Mr. Loaring-Clark consecrated the cornerstone of the new sanctuary. But the building was nearly complete, the new heating plant was working perfectly, and the 250 attendees were inside for the hour-long ceremony. There was no furniture yet, so all stood. First, Herbert

Jordan, senior warden, placed numerous articles in a large copper and tin box. A history written by the Rector; a silver dollar (indicating gifts); a Bible; the Prayer book; a hand-drawn and illuminated map of the church location; a packet of parsley seeds for the watching associate rector; and a copy of *The Commercial Appeal* in which the cornerstone ceremony was announced. Henry Lancaster, chairman of the Building Committee, used a portable flame unit to seal the box by soldering the top shut. Everyone processed outside, where The Rev. Mr. Loaring-Clark symbolically sealed the cornerstone—using snow instead of mortar.

On March 14, 1949, the Rector wrote to the architect:

". . . the grace of lines, the conformation of the arches, the wheel windows, the barrel ceiling, and the exceedingly harmonious conformation of both the exterior and

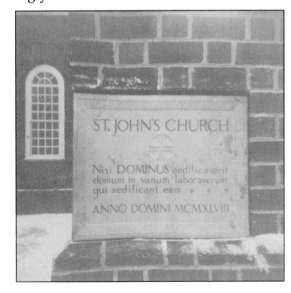

1949

the interior of the church . . . are meaningful. . . . I know that the Nicene Creed, the service of Holy Communion, the music of Bach, a congregation kneeling to receive the absolution—to be most meaningful, must have a setting which certainly is not a lovely little Congregational meeting house. . . . Our new church interior should be the best

The most gratifying thing in life is to look back over your shoulder [with] the knowledge that we have done well some things which bless others than ourselves."

job possible to proclaim the devoutness of the Church, while throwing around the worshipper what Dr. Otto calls 'the idea of the numenous.' Mystery cannot be excluded from worship as it can be from a lecture at the Goodwyn Institute." Mr. Loaring-Clark also wrote to thank the Building Committee—and especially Mr. Herbert Jordan—for staying with the project since "those days when there was little money, not too much faith [in the viability of the

---

DEAN AND CHAPTER OF CANTERBURY

2nd September, 1949.

Dear Sir:

On behalf of the Dean and Chapter of Canterbury, I am pleased to inform you that your letter to them was read and acted on favorably. The piece of stone for your Altar was handed to your representative, Mr. Fergus O'Connor, last week. We trust it will meet your requirements.

Yours truly,

Reginald Tophill
(Chapter Agent)

The Rev. Alfred Loaring-Clark,
Memphis, Tennessee.

St. John's Episcopal Church Bulletin, 1949

building project], and an immense number of problems to be solved. . . . The most gratifying thing in life is to look back over your shoulder [with] the knowledge that we have done well some things which bless others than ourselves."

The new building was ready in time for Palm Sunday services on April 10th. It was a joyous occasion.

The new church was consecrated on May 22, in the dramatic order of service for the Consecration from the Prayer Book. The Rt. Rev. Edmund P. Dandridge, D.D., Bishop of Tennessee, officiated and delivered the sermon. As hundreds of parishioners sat in silence in the new building, the Bishop walked up to the door, knocked three times, identified himself when asked, and stated that the purpose of his visit was "To consecrate this new church building to the glory of God who, in all his creation and especially in Christ Jesus our Lord, has revealed His greatness, His majesty, and His eternal love." With trumpet fanfare and the choir singing "Gloria in excelsis Deo," the Bishop and Canon James R. Sharpe as his attending Chaplain entered the new church. Mr. T. K. Robinson, senior warden, presented the church building to the Diocese of Tennessee in the name of the congregation of St. John's— a debt-free building worthy to be consecrated.

Wednesday, August 10, 1949 - Vestry Minutes

Mr. Loaring-Clark told of a letter he had received from the Archbishop of Canterbury, setting out that the Archbishop of Canterbury had agreed to send a stone from the oldest church in England, his church, from which a cross will be hewed and placed in the permanent altar when it is built. The stone, from an

My dear People:

As we move on Palm Sunday morning from our old church building to our beautiful new one, I beg most earnestly for your loyalty, your consecration and the faithful performance of your religious duties.

I lay on your consciences the need of our Parish for a happy enthusiasm and willing determination to bridge the psychological gap between our small, lovely and quaint little building and the light, roomy and different new interior. Surely our Sunday morning worship in the new church building will seem different. The transition can be made successfully and with no emotional disturbance if we go into our new building prepared for a change, and determined to grow into an appreciation of the new, as we have of the old.

I can imagine nothing more devastating to the morale and courage of our congregation than services in our new church poorly attended. For your Parish's sake, resolve for the next three months to let nothing prevent your attendance in our new church. If our congregation will do this, the transition from the old setting to the new will find us with more enthusiasm -- not less.

Space permits me to mention only briefly a second most important matter. I have been conscious for five years of a sad omission in my pastoral duties. It has weighed heavily on my conscience as your leader, yet lack of space in our church building has prevented my doing anything about it. It is the most important matter of PARENTS BRINGING THEIR CHILDREN TO CHURCH with them.

If the religious training of our children is our most important duty as parents, we neglect it only at the peril of our children's future. We TAKE our children to the circus but either leave them at home or SEND them to church. Why?

Children in the first three grades should attend church with mother and father at least once in the month. In the fourth and fifth grades they should be in church almost every Sunday with their parents. In the sixth grade they are normally confirmed and then assume their own obligations of church attendance. Beginning on Palm Sunday and continuing through the life of our Parish I intend to hold up the ideal of family worship as a normal element in our Christian living. There will be no excuse for me as your Rector, nor for you as communicants and parents, now that we have adequate space in which our Parish families can worship.

No one is quite so thrilled or grateful to God for our beautiful new church as I am. I want in every possible way to make the transition from old to new a beautiful, emotionally strong and radiant experience.

With kindest personal regards I am most cordially, your friend and Rector,

Alfred Loaring-Clark

11th century Norman Altar, would be the center of five similar stones, cut with the five traditional crosses. He said that he hoped to have five crosses, representing the five wounds of Christ, in stones from Antioch, Palestine, Rome, and Cairo—the five great centers of Christianity—and they are all to be utilized as the one from Canterbury.

In November 1951, Mr. Loaring-Clark reported that Miss Ann Buckner Potts had recently returned from Rome with a stone from the Basilica of St. Sebastian for St. John's future altar.

February 8, 1950 - Vestry Minutes

The Vestry approved ordering brick for the new wing and for steps and entrance to the North Chapel. Sound equipment would be tried out for the two dead spots in the church. A communicant offered to pay half of the cost of air conditioning the church if St. John's would pay the other half. In April the Vestry Minutes record that Mr. Sanders decided to give $5,000 on the air conditioning, instead of just half.

Thanks from the Vestry to many people prove that the new location was a project involving the whole Parish.

Among people thanked were Mrs. Paul Mueller for planting and Mrs. Percy Parker for work on the new wing.

Some smaller projects such as putting a door on a closet and some weatherstripping were postponed for budget reasons.

In February 1950, Mr. Parsley accepted a call to the Canterbury Club at Vanderbilt University. The search for a new associate rector began, and The Rev. Mr. Wallace Pennepacker came from New Jersey to St. John's.

On November 7, 1951, the Vestry voted to accept an offer from East Memphis Lions Club to purchase the property at Semmes and Spottswood for $7,500, to be paid $1,000 cash and $500 annually at 5% interest.

First Palm Sunday at Central and Greer, 1949

January 16, 1952 - Annual Meeting
In his report to the parish, Russell C. Gregg, President, drew a visual as well as a financial illustration of the progress:

"The contrast between our present plant and the modest quarters which we occupied at Semmes and Spottswood represents a remarkable achievement in a comparatively short period of time, and at the same time places a responsibility upon each and every one of us to see that the obligations which we have assumed to make this transformation possible are discharged on time and without default. Our total expenditure in buildings alone totals $377,064.03. In addition, we

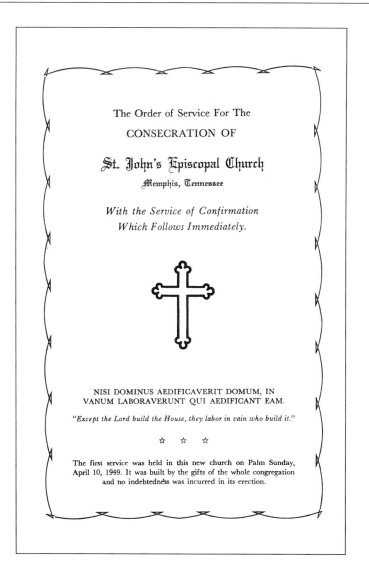

The Order of Service For The

CONSECRATION OF

St. John's Episcopal Church
Memphis, Tennessee

With the Service of Confirmation Which Follows Immediately.

NISI DOMINUS AEDIFICAVERIT DOMUM, IN VANUM LABORAVERUNT QUI AEDIFICANT EAM.

"Except the Lord build the House, they labor in vain who build it."

☆ ☆ ☆

The first service was held in this new church on Palm Sunday, April 10, 1949. It was built by the gifts of the whole congregation and no indebtedness was incurred in its erection.

have a very fine pipe organ as a memorial gift, representing an investment of more than $25,000, pews at $11,000, and miscellaneous equipment, both bought and transferred from our former location, which is estimated to be worth some $20,000. We have completed, and have in process, mural decorations, which, when finished, will represent between $15,000 and $20,000 in intrinsic value. All of the above, together with the land value on which the church is located, represents the fiscal assets of the corporation; against this there is a funded debt of $175,000, requiring amortization payments of $15,812 annually. . . . The officers and directors of the Corporation feel that our building program must pause where it is until our indebtedness is liquidated."

St. John's Episcopal Church
Central and Greer
Memphis 11, Tennessee
October 21, 1949

Rev. Alfred Loaring-Clark, D. D., Rector
2945 Southern Avenue

Rev. Henry Nutt Parsley, Associate
3254 Central Avenue
3254 Central

Mrs. Ed Newell
3220 Seminole
Memphis, Tennessee

My dear Frances:

This morning's mail brings a check from Celeste and Herbert Vaiden in memory of your dear mother. Of course, I have thanked them for their gift. They asked that it be placed in the Building Fund.

I know you will be pleased and touched by their thoughtfulness.

With kindest personal regard to you and Ed, I am

Always yours,

Tib

AL-C:mdc

Frances, Please call the office and give me your mother's full name before Tuesday morning so that I may list this in the Memorial column for the Bulletin.
Mel

October 21, 1949

February, 1951

Summer, 1951

*M*rs. Elizabeth Saunders Ramsay's history of St. John's, written in 1938, states that when Mr. and Mrs. Lehman Johnson and their four-year-old daughter Mary moved to Buntyn in 1907, Mrs. Johnson became organist for the little hand-pumped organ. When the Palmer Farnsworth family came five years later, Mrs. Farnsworth led in singing the hymns. There were not enough members to have a choir until about 1915. When Mr. and Mrs. Phil Hacker moved to the growing mission church, Mr. Hacker sometimes accompanied the choir with his cornet.

As the mission again became a parish with The Rev. Mr. Loaring-Clark as Rector, the music program increased.

St. John's Children's Choir

The Rev. Mr. Loaring-Clark loved music and worked to enhance the church's music. Mr. James E. Morrison served briefly as organist in 1929-30, then Mrs. Forest McGinley accepted the job. Carolyn "Ursi" McGinley had begun playing for church services when she was 10 years old. She had four years' experience as an organist-choirmas-

> **"The deep tones of the Laura Sharpe Memorial Organ resounded throughout the neighborhood of St. John's Episcopal Church during the midnight service on Christmas Eve. . . . Mrs. Laura Sharpe died at her home two doors away from the church a few minutes later."**

ter when she accepted the responsibility at St. John's. Mrs. Forest McGinley remained for 16 years in loyal and effective service, resigning at the end of 1946.

In 1936, a new Hammond organ was installed as a memorial to Mrs. Laura Elam Sharp, whose family had nurtured the mission through decades. A newspaper article says that the person who most wanted to hear the new organ was not present. "The deep tones of the Laura Sharpe Memorial Organ resounded throughout the neighborhood of St. John's Episcopal Church during the midnight service on Christmas Eve. . . . Mrs. Laura Sharpe died at her home two doors away from the church a few minutes later." She had been too ill to attend, and, at age 82, was also deaf. But she remembered when Miss Cary Watkins—although a Presbyterian and not a member of St. John's—had played the pump organ for services in the late 1870s.

A newspaper article from 1937 tells of St. John's choir presenting a special vespers service at St. Luke's Episcopal Church in Jackson, Tennessee, by invitation from The Rev. Dr. W. J. Loaring-Clark. In addition to the program, which included works by Bach, Tchaikowsky, Mozart, Rossini, Palestrina, and others, the article lists choir members:

Sopranos - Lucille Allen, Ruby Edmiston, Ruth Loaring-Clark, Margaret Martin, Ruth Metcalfe, Frances McPeak, Rosemary York, Mrs. Fred Beacham (who was also choir mother), Mme. Louise Bowen, Mrs. Jess Hall, Mrs. Gilbert January, Mrs. Walter Lott, Mrs. William E. Oates, and Mrs. H. J. Wasson.

Contraltos - Martha Lawton, Laura Russell, Margaret Sammons, Mary Jo Tate, Mrs. Raynor Allen, Mrs. Ronald Hopton, Mrs. Dick McCool, Mrs. Paul Ramsey, and Mrs. John Worth.

Tenors - Barney Fields, Mallory Morris, Francis McGee, Milton McGrew, and Forrest McGinley.

Bassos - Raynor Allen, C. A. Arthur, George Claiborne, R. P. Graves, Edward Hawtrey, Ronald Hopton, and Sam Lowry.

The church sponsored Mrs. McGinley to attend summer music school in Colorado for 21 days in the summer of 1939. The Vestry approved her buying for the choir "the very expensive Oxford Press Anthem books" in 1940. They also approved spending $10 to give the annual party for the choir, held at the W. G. Abbott home. Mrs. McGinley reported to the Vestry in the fall of 1940 that 17 members of St. John's choir were also members of Memphis Symphony Orchestra choir—the most representation of any church in the city.

For a worship service at The Shell on July 10, 1943

...in the fall of 1940 that 17 members of St. John's choir were also members of Memphis Symphony Orchestra choir—the most representation of any church in the city.

Mrs. McGinley chose "God be in my Head" (Davies) among other pieces for the 28-voice choir to sing. It continues to be programmed by church choirs, although church music, like other forms, has trends.

In March 1944, Dr. Burnet Tuthill, professor in the Music Department at Southwestern College (now named Rhodes College), became Chairman of the Music Committee, reporting to the Vestry not only the status of the choir, but suggesting ways to improve the music program.

In 1945, the Kenneth Duncans made a generous gift toward purchasing new hymnals, so that there would be enough for the growing congregation.

At Mrs. McGinley's retirement, Fergus O'Connor "came by plane from Queen's College, Oxford, England" to be organist/choirmaster and also to be on faculty at the College of Music at Southwestern. The son of a professional musician, he studied under the organist at Chichester Cathedral at age 18, was appointed assistant one year later, and kept the position for five years. For two years, he held a position at a church in Oxford as organist/choirmaster, then went to London where he directed a chorus of 120 boys. He was in the Army, then went back to Oxford as organist/director of music at Queen's College. He also had taught at Summer Fields, a boy's prep school for Eton. He came highly recommended to St. John's.

In July 1947, Mr. O'Connor told the Vestry that he was "desirous of organizing a Boys' Choir," and that 20 children already had volunteered to join such a Choir; that after the boys received proper instructions, it was planned to have them join in the Sunday Services and sing with the regular choir and also sing carols at Christmas. Further, that a plan would be worked out for the boys to be given an incentive by way of making pocket money for

St. John's Children's Choir

regular attendance and attention to duties. The Vestry was unanimous in its approval of the plan and pledged its whole-hearted support to it.

Just six months later, Mr. John Stout, Music Committee Chairman, reported that he had received many favorable comments on the boys' choir. Following general discussion about this choir and church music in general, the Vestry voted unanimously to allocate the necessary funds for payments to members of the boys' choir. Two months later the Vestry increased the Music Committee's allowance for the 1948 budget.

Mr. Stout reported in March that there were now 26 boys in the boys' choir, with a waiting list from which to replace several boys who would graduate. Thirty boys attended the Music Appreciation Class. He also announced that the Cantata to be held at the Cathedral on April 25th would be sung entirely by St. John's choir.

Fergus O'Connor with the Boys' Choir, 1947

Mr. Jay Smith was requested to give a report at the next meeting on the comparison of the Lenten choir attendance with that of previous years so that consideration could be given as to whether the Lenten choir should be continued as a separate organization or whether it should be merged with the boys' choir.

By mid-1948 the music program seemed highly successful in several directions. The Vestry agreed that the success of the Cantata rated establishing several performances each year, and that the Women's Auxiliary should be asked to sponsor the programs. They also voted to raise Mr. O'Connor's salary to $2,500.

Once again, the church needed a better organ, and Mr. O'Connor was sent to St. Louis to try out a possible purchase, for approximately $10,000. When the new organ was selected, it was built by a different company and was a gift to the parish by Mr. and Mrs. Herbert Humphreys. The old organ was sold for $800.

The Women's Auxiliary decided in April 1949 to include the Boys' Choir in their projects. When Meade Nichol was interviewed in the early 1970s, she reminisced about her sons Dick and Lytle being in the choir, and Fergus O'Connor giving them a knowledge and love of good music. Mr. O'Connor took most of the boys who were in the choir to England at one point. He did ask that the Vestry pay any expenses he incurred for the Boys' Choir, and they voted an increase of $20 per month.

Another Cantata was planned for October 1948, and the Women's Auxiliary agreed to help underwrite the expense.

St. John's Children's Choir processing into the sanctuary, 1950

Just when the music program seemed especially successful, differences over management of the Boys' Choir led to Fergus O'Connor's resignation.

For a few brief months, Vernon Perdue Davis, on the faculty of Memphis College of Music at Southwestern, became new choirmaster at St. John's. He held an M.A. from Princeton, specializing in musical composition. He had experience as a master at Woodberry Forest School in Virginia and was choirmaster at St. Andrew's Chapel there. But conflict between his academic duties and church responsibilities resulted in only a short stay, although the Vestry agreed with Dr. Tuthill that they would continue Mr. Davis' salary through the spring semester.

This time, the Vestry was most impressed with a hometown musician who had been living and studying in New York. He was Richard White, who won the gold medal for having the highest marks in his graduating class at the Guilmant Organ School in New York. He also received an associate degree from the American Guild of Organists. He later told a newspaper interviewer that he was surprised to learn that the church for which he played, St. Matthew's Lutheran Church in Manhattan, was founded "before Johann Sebastian Bach was born."

Richard White

During World War II he served with the Army Air Corps in the South Pacific. Before returning to Memphis he was organist for an Episcopal church in New Jersey.

In August 1950 the Vestry voted to engage Richard White as organist/choir director at a salary of $275 per month, with a future arrangement of $25 per month auto allowance. Norfleet Turner made a motion that up to $250 moving expense be paid by St. John's. Mr. Russell Gregg was designated to make housing arrangements for Mr. White and for the new associate rector, Mr. Pennepacker. Richard and Mahaffey White found a house on Central, very near the church, and the Vestry agreed to buy it, with a lease-option arrangement for the Whites. Richard White was organist/choirmaster for 36 years, until his retirement in 1986.

There were differences of opinion about the music program; there was sometimes dissension among parishioners or choir members about what type of music the choir should present. There were periods of difficulty in gaining the kind of commitment from singers that would permit difficult works to be presented, although some choir members were loyal for years. In 1953 Mrs. Fred Beacham was presented a letter of appreciation for 18 years in the choir. But Mr. White reported to the Vestry that he could only count on 13-15 people, when he really needed 30-40 choir members. Through it

ST. JOHN'S EPISCOPAL CHURCH - CHOIR OF BOYS & GIRLS - MARCH 15, 1966
RICHARD T. WHITE - ORGANIST & CHOIRMASTER

Richard White and the Lenten Choir, 1966

all, Richard White gained acclaim from his peers and a reputation as a fine musician. He played a special service of choral and organ music to mark the 25th anniversary that he and The Rev. Mr. Wallace M. Pennepacker had served St. John's. He composed a special setting of the Beatitudes for the Centennial celebration in 1978. And he traded witty barbs written in doggerel with The Rev. Mr. Alfred Loaring-Clark. Once when the Rector kiddingly complained that the processional music was not long enough, Richard White wrote back, in verse, that if

Mr. Loaring-Clark walked a little faster, the timing would work out.

A boys' and girls' choir originated in 1953, to sing for the new summer service at 9:30. By 1970 the adult choir had again grown but the boys' and girls' choir dwindled (as did the church school) as a result of the declining birth rate that began in the early 1960s. The children's choir was discontinued in 1973, but re-formed for Christmas, Lent, and Easter.

Richard White and the Lenten Choir, early 1970s

Through the turbulent decades of the 1960s and 1970s the consensus fluctuated about appropriate music for worship. Folk idiom, more contemporary compositions, and less formal structure were some of the ideas proposed for church music. By 1971, the Vestry was discussing whether choir members should be paid, since some churches had adopted such a policy.

Other musicians among the parishioners provided leadership for musical groups. Jack Abell, Ann and Dick Reynolds, Sandra and Don Freund, and Dr. Burnet Tuthill

St. John's Adult Choir, 1980s

were among the people who directed a part of the church's music program through changing forms for worship music. The Children's Orff Choir was one of the activities that lasted for a few years. One of the longer lasting groups was the Lenten Choir, which in 1952 attracted 72 youngsters.

The Lenten Choir, started by Irene Beasley, grew to 92 participants in the mid-1940s. Children from about the age of eight to early teens rehearsed three afternoons each week during Lent. They learned prayers and hymns. Each Sunday afternoon they sang a half-hour evensong, vested

The first city-wide choir service, Festival Evensong, 1960

in the traditional black cassock and white cotta with the girls wearing a small black cap. The choir organized on Ash Wednesday and climaxed on Easter Sunday. Those who came regularly (or made up a few missed times) and learned the required materials earned a silver cross the first year. The second year they were awarded gold crosses for participation. An amethyst was added for each year of service. Diana Carr Bailey remembers that Lenten Choir was fun and that she and her friends treasured the crosses they received.

Richard White says that this was a favorite project

Christmas, 1945

of The Rev. Mr. Loaring-Clark, and he always asked the name of any children he didn't know, promised to call them by name the next time he saw them, or give them a dime for their mite box if he could not remember.

Many of the acolytes came from the Lenten Choir.

St. John's presented the "Bethlehem" nativity play just before Christmas from 1950 until it was discontinued in 1963.

Written in elegant language by Laurence Housman, "Bethlehem" was performed in costume by 28 adults and one child. Mrs. Loaring-Clark (Clara) persuaded Mahaffey

Reeds contribute vibrancy and color of the sound.

White to undertake making the costumes, with some help. The materials came from a large house on East Parkway where the draperies were being taken down—velvet material lined and inner-lined. Many of the play's lines were Biblical passages and gave a meaningful experience to those who participated and to those who saw the performance. The adult choir provided the occasional music with words from the text.

The present organ at St. John's was built by the M. P. Moller Company of Hagerstown, Maryland. The original gift from Mr. and Mrs. Herbert Humphreys was a memorial to his parents, Hugh and Flournoy Selden Humphreys. It consisted of a console of three manuals (or keyboards) of five octaves each and a pedalboard of two and a half octaves with flue pipes that form the main body of the organ. In 1971, a further gift in memory of Mr. Humphreys' sister, Elise Humphreys Race, and brother, Selden Humphreys, added reed pipes.

The flue pipes create the basic organ sound, including the Diapason or Principal characteristic organ sound, flutes, and strings, with mixtures made possible by stops and couplers. Reeds contribute vibrancy and color of the sound. The Humphreys' gift in 1971 brought the organ to 2,094 pipes, with the wind supply provided by a 10 horsepower motor. Additions since 1971 added more color, especially a big trumpet stop. Reuter took over the organ and totally rebuilt it in 1990 when the church was renovated. There are now about 45 sets of pipes, called "ranks."

With Richard White's retirement, after more than three and one-half decades during which church music changed more rapidly than at any other time in history, John P. Ayer, Jr. came to St. John's a week later.

Born in Boston, reared just outside Chicago in Winnetka, Illinois, John Ayer went back east to school. He took his Bachelor of Music degree at Hartt College of Music in Hartford, Connecticut. He then earned two graduate degrees from SMU in Dallas: an M.A. in both Organ Performance and in Church Music. Next came an assistantship at Canterbury Cathedral. He then became Chapel Organist and Director of Choral Activities at Tabor Academy in southeastern Massachusetts. He pursued a doctorate degree in Organ Performance and Choral Conducting at Eastman School of Music in Rochester, New York, before coming to St. John's in 1986.

During his 10 years he has carried forward the tradition of great church music. He also has directed the Memphis Boy Choir, which has gained international acclaim from touring and compact disc recordings. Although the group is not affiliated with St. John's as was

Nativity scene, 1956

Participants in "The Mikado"

the previous Boys' Choir under Fergus O'Connor, they are associated with the church in the minds of the public through both their director and their performances there.

The Memphis Boy Choir was established under the auspices of St. John's as an outreach program, although it is independent musically. Few members of the choir are also members of the church. The group does rehearse at the church, and regularly sings services of choral Evensong. John Ayer also established Memphis Chamber Choir, an adult counterpart to the Boy Choir, enabling the combined group to sing SATB (four-part) literature. Both groups tour and record as independent musical organizations, now under independent non-profit charter.

St. John's has consistently sponsored concerts, especially such highlights as the Reynolds family's concert during the week of the 1978 Centennial Celebration. Other music organizations frequently use the sanctuary for performances because of the admirable acoustics—gained after great difficulty and consultations when the building was new.

For eight years during the late 1930s and early 1940s, a group of troupers at St. John's produced the Annual

Evening Operetta. Marian Scrivener wrote that it was originally a simple talent show, but grew into such ambitious productions as *The Mikado* and *H.M.S. Pinafore*. Apparently, Raynor Allen was a Gilbert and Sullivan buff who wanted the annual event to exceed the previous one. With his coaching, a cast and crew of all ages painted over the previous year's sets, practiced with Margaret Dallas accompanying them on piano, and gave spirited performances. Frances Dallas was the scenery specialist. She sketched the scenery on a backdrop of heavy domestic sized with Sears Best water-based white paint. Young people in the church shared in the fun of painting, and helped to hang the wavy backdrop from hooks in the ceiling. Reminiscences sound as if St. John's offered competition to the Memphis Open Air Theatre operetta productions at The Shell in Overton Park. All this without a real stage.

> *Another thing—yea, one thing more:*
> *I'll grant processionals are a bore*
> *And hymns have stanzas without end*
> *So many, mayhap, they could send*
> *An organist to kingdom come*
> *If he were listless, stupid, dumb.*
> *I'm just the Rector—heaven forbid*
> *That I should tell our music kid*
> *Just what he should or should not do.*
> *Yet 'twould be helpful if we knew*
> *Just when a hymn can end with grace*
> *And still have Clergy in their place.*
> *— A. L-C.*

THE CRUSADERS OF THE CROSS
ST. JOHN'S EPISCOPAL CHURCH
Memphis, Tennessee

Present

THE MIKADO

W. S. Gilbert - - - Sir Arthur Sullivan

Under the Direction of
Mr. Raynor Allen

Chorus Direction	Miss Marian Scrivener
Stage Setting	Miss Frances Dallas and Miss Marian Scrivener
Overture—Piano Duet from The Mikado	
	Elaine Berry and Mary Virginia Burchett

CAST OF CHARACTERS

THE MIKADO, Ruler of Japan	Felder Morehead
NANKI-POO, His Son, Disguised as a Wandering Minstrel	Denleigh Clarke
KO-KO, Lord High Executioner of Titipu	Jack Lancaster
POOH-BAH, Lord High Everything Else	Louie Burt, Jr.
PISH-TUSH, a Noble Lord	Sammy Cone
YUM-YUM	Margaret Loring-C'ark
PITTI-SING	Jean Fox
PEEP-BO	Mary Virginia Burchett
KATISHA, an Elderly Lady in Love with Nanki-Poo	Clara Mae Scrivener

(YUM-YUM, PITTI-SING, PEEP-BO: Three Sisters, Wards of Ko-Ko)

NOBLES:

George Howell   Robert Ring

CHORUS:

Jeanne Abbott	Ann Allen
Reta Anderson	Elaine Berry
Martha Lee Crawford	Martha Dabney
Mary Gideon	Jean Hazlehurst
Virginia Jones	Sarah Loring-Clark

TIME: In Old Japan

PLACE: Garden of Ko-Ko's Residence

The Crusaders acknowledge with gratitude:

Mr. Allen's expert direction and entertaining interpretations of Gilbert and Sullivan, which have made our rehearsals delightful;

The assistance of Crusader Alumni, Martha Dabney, Mary Gideon, Jean Hazlehurst, Denleigh Clarke, Jack Lancaster and Felder Morehead, without which the production would have been impossible;

The services of our charming ticket taker and former president, Helen Shawhan;

The use of a genuine Mandarin robe for the Mikado, through the kindness of Mrs. Wm. D. Anderson;

The never-failing support of our parents and friends.

———

We call your attention to sale of Coca-Cola by the Senior League—candy by the Crusaders.

The Murals

12

The murals in St. John's were painted by Jan Hendrik de Rosen, who was born in Warsaw, Poland and reared in France. His father was a painter for the last two czars of Russia, specializing in great scenes of battles.

John de Rosen (as his name became in America) swung a scaffold before a bare brick wall, charged with turning it into a 12 by 14 painting during his month-long stay.

First, plasterers covered the bricks. Then, the artist made the surface ready for the paint (telling art critic Guy Northrop that the process was secret). He used a kind of

"... like watercolor, transparent; it won't chip or flake."

wax tempera, which, he said, was "like watercolor, transparent; it won't chip or flake." He made a tiny sketch of his idea, put one vertical and one horizontal line across the surface to establish balance, made a charcoal sketch on the wall, and began painting. He was 58 years old when he painted the Madonna and Child.

He said that every face in his murals was a portrait, because the reality of a live face establishes contact between the viewer and the mural. Sometimes he used a parishioner as a model for part of a drawing—the hair, hands, posture—and people who watched him work relate that he also used reference books to ensure that elements in his paintings were appropriate to the period.

In all, he painted nine murals for St. John's (eight in the Sanctuary and one in the working Sacistry), in less than two years.

... every face in his murals was a portrait...

But the work that gave him his start as a muralist took five years to complete. He covered the entire interior of the Cathedral of Lwow, in his native Poland.

He was Professor of Drawing and Monumental Composition at the Institute of Technology of Lwow, following his education at the universities of Lausanne, Munich, and Paris. He was on the faculty of the Catholic University of America, Washington, D.C., from 1939 to 1949, where he occupied the chair of Research Professor of Liturgical Art.

Chosen by Pope Pius XI to paint the murals in the Pope's private chapel at Castelgondolfo, he was the first artist chosen to decorate a pontifical chapel since Michaelangelo created the frescoes of the Sistine Chapel.

His honors vary from the Golden Laurel of the Polish Academy of Literature (1938) to the French Legion of Honor, French War Cross, British Military Medal, Virtuti

Militari Cross for Valor, and international painting commissions.

The listing of his body of work includes paintings in 10 states and in Austria, Italy, and Poland. He also designed stained glass windows in his native country in the 1930's; unfortunately, many were destroyed by war in 1939. His murals and decoration of King Sobieski Chapel,

He gained recognition in <u>Who's Who in American Art.</u>

Kahlenberg, Vienna, Austria, were classified as a National Monument in 1930. He gained recognition in *Who's Who in American Art.*

When the artist first arrived in Memphis to paint, he returned to California without having been able to really begin the mural. The wall was plastered, ready for painting—but refused to dry. Work was postponed until the following spring.

Christ Triumphant
(over the High Altar)

The idea for the mural over the high altar was suggested by The Reverend Mr. Loaring-Clark, depicting the first line from one of his favorite hymns, "Christ the fair glory of the holy angels." Angels were created by God to act as His messengers.

In the mural the resurrected Christ stands with arms outstretched in an attitude of blessing. One is reminded of the sinewy arms in Leonardo da Vinci's drawing "The Proportions of Man," although the elongated figure in the mural is not proportioned like the 1509 drawing. In the mural His head is surrounded by a nimbus, symbolizing

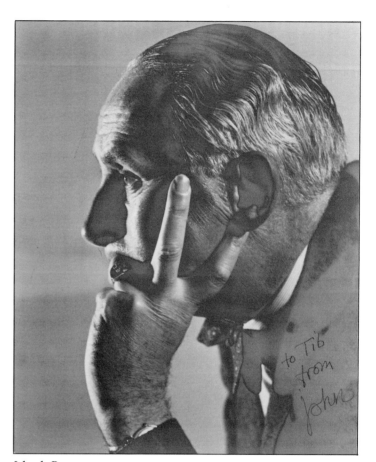

John de Rosen

divinity. The cross is behind him, and he is no longer nailed to it. Two circles behind him represent the universe, with stars showing the constellations of the western hemisphere in spring. The messenger angels on each side hold incense burners, symbolizing the purification of the Son. The angels are turned toward Christ, but not entirely away from Heaven.

The red background of the mural symbolizes power and love.

St. John the Evangelist, patron of the church, stands below Christ. In the tradition of the early Church, St. John is represented as an old man, apocalyptic author of the

Revelation, rather than the Beloved Disciple depicted in later Christian art. St. John was the only apostle who lived to be old and who died a natural death.

Two medallions above him represent the four evangelists, Luke and John on the left, Mark and Matthew on the right. The symbols in the medallions represent the four dominant characteristics of the Savior. Matthew's symbol is a winged man, signifying the humanity of Christ. Mark's symbol, a winged lion, denotes kingship of Christ. Luke's

John's symbol, a winged eagle, represents the divinity of Christ.

symbol is a winged ox denoting sacrifice. John's symbol, a winged eagle, represents the divinity of Christ.

The six blue wings represent the cherubim, who guard the throne, described in the Revelation. Archangels stand on each side of St. John. From left to right, they are: JOPHIEL, who, according to tradition, drove Adam and Eve from Paradise and protected the gates of Eden with a flaming sword, a symbol of God's judgment. His shield shows Adam and Eve and the Tree of Knowledge. The serpent is under his foot, showing that Satan will be overcome. The jewels in his wings are moonstones which, according to the symbolism of the Middle Ages, are the symbol of marriage. CHAMUEL, who tradition credits with having stood by Christ in the agony of the Garden of Gethsemane. He holds a symbolic chalice, a reminder of Christ's prayer, "Let this cup pass from me." The chalice is a reproduction of an early chalice that is in the treasury of the Basilica of St. Mark in Venice. The gem of Chamuel is the amethyst, as shown on his wings. The purple of the garment

Christ Triumphant

symbolizes mourning, sorrow, and penance.

URIEL, who is the archangel of light, the regent of the sun, and the keeper of beauty. He holds a Greek column, which symbolizes the perfection in aesthetics. The staff he carries is topped with the sun, because he is the regent of the constellations. Uriel's gem is the emerald. His robe is the color of fire, one of the simple substances (earth, water, air, and fire) early regarded as constituting the material universe.

MICHAEL, God's special angel, who is the leader of the angels in the fight against the devil. As the flagbearer of the Church Militant, he is dressed in armor with the sharp-pointed sword of God's judgment in hand, and the crown of victory on his head. On his breastplate he is shown piercing the devil with his lance, according to an early Greek icon. His gem is the ruby, the color of blood, a symbol of the fighter and of Christ's blood shed for the church.

GABRIEL, who is the Holy Messenger and the archangel of the Annunciation. The scene of the Annunciation, when he

The Annunciation mural at St. John's reflects this early tradition of iconography.

appeared to Mary to tell her she has been chosen to birth the Christchild, is shown embroidered on his white cloak. He is holding the triple rose, which until the 14th century was the symbol of the Blessed Virgin. His gem is the sapphire.

RAPHAEL, who is the protector of traveling youth, the friend and defender of young Tobias, whom he saved from the monster that wanted to devour him. He is shown with his usual symbols in his hand, the pilgrim's staff and the fish. On the staff is the gourd, which travelers always carried so that they could drink from the springs. The two scallop shells that appear on his wings were the sign of pilgrims in the Middle Ages.

The clouds in the mural reflect the style of Albrecht Dürer, whose etchings greatly influenced de Rosen.

"Therefore with angels and archangels and all the company of heaven..."
-Preface to the Sanctus

This mural was presented by Mr. and Mrs. Norfleet Turner and Mr. and Mrs. Bayard Boyle, to the Glory of God and in loving memory of Mr. and Mrs. Samuel Ragland, parents of Mrs. Turner and Mrs. Boyle.

The Annunciation
Lady Chapel – South Transcept

The first image of the Annunciation is a fresco in the catacomb of Santa Praxeda, in Rome. It is probably of the second century, among the paintings in the catacombs made during the first to third centuries that are the earliest Christian images known. It shows the Blessed Virgin dipping water from a stream, and an angel approaching. The Annunciation mural at St. John's reflects this early tradition of iconography. Mary is receiving the word from Gabriel, the Holy Messenger, that she has been chosen to bear a special Son. She is dressed in white and pink—a pale and delicate virgin like a Fra Filippo Lippi Madonna. Gabriel's white robe symbolizes purity, with a golden belt for chastity, and a fiery red cloak symbolizing the Holy Ghost. He holds the traditional staff or sceptre, as in the

Christ Triumphant

Holy Mother Enthroned

The Annunciation

The Visitation

Baptism of Christ by St. John the Baptist in the Waters of Jordan

St. Paul at Corinth Baptizing St. Priscilla

Baptism of St. Augustine by His Teacher, St. Ambrose, Bishop of Milan

Christ the Judge

Byzantine tradition. The vase standing near the brook is a Syriac vessel of the first century, probably very similar to the vases used in Galilee at the time. The landscape is bare and rocky, an image of the outside world, but the Blessed Virgin is kneeling on a green meadow covered with spring flowers. The rays of light symbolizes the Holy Spirit descending on the Blessed Virgin.

The mural was given in memory of Gertrude Alcorn Russell by Mrs. Percy Wood, Mrs. Giles Coors, and Mr. Edward Russell.

The Visitation

This painting depicts the visit of Mary to her cousin, Elizabeth. Although advanced in age, Elizabeth and Zacharias were awaiting the birth of their first child, who was John the Baptist. Mary is dressed in white for purity. On her breast is a cross foretelling the sorrow that will come to her. Only two colors—blue and white, the colors of the Virgin—are used in this mural. This is the only one of the murals with such a simple palette. The mountains in the background represent the "hill country," Elizabeth's home. In Eastern iconography, a drapery generally denotes a human dwelling or house; the drapery and porch shown indicate Elizabeth's home.

This mural was given by Mrs. James Dinkins Robinson.

Holy Mother Enthroned

This mural depicts the Holy Mother, with arms outstretched, and the Christ Child, whose hand is raised in blessing, seated in her lap. On each side stand angels. The one to her right is offering a white falcon, or tercel, called the Bird of Kings and the King of Birds. He is rising to life again, symbol of the flier whose memory is honored by the painting. The angel to the left of the Holy Mother stands bidding the congregation to worship. The throne on which our Lady is seated is surrounded by rocks, with mountain peaks in the distance. Above and behind is an

. . . the murals depict three different customs at baptism.

immense night sky filled with stars.

In his dissertation on the murals, David Fox Taylor discusses the complexity of composition in this image, and compares landscape elements to those in works by Leonardo da Vinci, Mantegna, Ghirlandajo, Bellini, and Durer.

This mural was presented by Mr. and Mrs. Jules Rozier, to the Glory of God and in loving memory of her son, James DuBose Swearengen, Jr.

Baptism of Christ by St. John the Baptist
in the Waters of the Jordan
(Chapel of the Holy Spirit – North Transept)

This chapel is also the Baptistry, and the murals depict three different customs at baptism.

The landscape in this mural is purely conventional, as are the waters of the river. Two unnamed figures in the foreground derive from early images of the baptism of our Lord, which show these two figures standing or kneeling, although they probably have no special significance.

The dove above is the symbol of the Holy Ghost, which appeared during the baptism.

The artist gave the figures rugged, muscular vigor. Like Mary in *The Annunciation*, Christ is blonde, in contrast to the disciples, but nothing like the pale asceticism in paintings such as the same subject by Piero della Francesca (15th century). The coloration of the figure unifies him with the landscape.

St. Paul at Corinth Baptizing St. Priscilla

The Greek ruins symbolize the dying pagan antiquity, but the baptismal waters from the Greek fountain create a link between the world of classical antiquity and Christianity. The other figures complete the aesthetic composition. This mural depicts baptism by aspersion (sprinkling the water) from a golden cup that St. Paul is holding in his right hand.

Baptism of St. Augustine by His Teacher, St. Ambrose, Bishop of Milan

This mural represents the beginning of the new Christian era, as St. Ambrose, a man of antiquity, baptizes Augustine, an architect of Christian civilization.

After the catacumins were baptized, they were given a cup of milk and honey. This custom disappeared very shortly after the 5th century. The mural shows St. Ambrose giving young Augustine, clad in a Roman patrician dalmatic, a silver cup containing the milk and honey.

Behind St. Augustine stands his mother, St. Monica, and a crucifer holding a bejeweled cross.

The background is the reproduction of a mural painting (probably of the early 6th century) depicting the ordination of St. Augustine by St. Ambrose. The figure of the archangel above is also the reproduction of a painting of the same period. The Roman lamp burning at the side of St. Ambrose is the symbol of learning and philosophy.

All of the murals in this chapel were given by Mr. and Mrs. Herbert Humphreys.

Christ the Judge
(West Wall)

Christ the Judge, is seated on a throne, symbol of authority. From his majestic figure radiates grace, transfusing the universe and lighting both the earth and moon under his feet. Behind the throne the archangel Gabriel holds the trumpet in readiness for the Day of Judgment.

Christ the Judge

Below, an angel holds the Book of Knowledge opened to the year 1953. The other angel holds the scales of justice on which are weighed the souls of men. The angel has no part in judging, so his eyes are closed. The equations are Einstein's theory of relativity,

The white spot represents Memphis.

announced in January 1950. The announcement article in *Time* called it "the most important scientific news in many decades" and Einstein called the four equations "an attempt to interrelate all known physical phenomena." The artist is saying that theology and science have the same source—God. The white spot represents Memphis.

Worshippers facing the mural over the High Altar, which represented the Risen Christ as triumphant over the whole creation, were reminded of Heaven. Therefore, the mural as we leave the church should remind us, not only of where we have been, but that we should take it with us into the world. Our worship was not to be something apart from everyday life, but the motivating force behind it. Indeed, we would be continually judged by the correspondence, or lack of it, between our worship and the quality of our lives at all times and in all places.

-The Reverend Mr. Wallace Pennepacker

This mural was given to the Glory of God and in memory of The Rev. Mr. Loaring-Clark by his friends.

To apply the paint to the wall, the artist used Ceracolors—a medium of basic natural colors dissolved in cold wax. When these paints became unavailable, he switched to casein paints. Both are unavailable today. Wherever there is gold leaf or imitation gold leaf, he used a different process. He applied slow size (a glutinous glaze that makes a smooth surface for the gold leaf). Eighteen hours later he applied sheets of gold leaf over the size. A statement from Mr. de Rosen confirms this (April 2, 1977).

-Phoebe Paxton Dent

In *Christ Triumphant*, the face of Jophiel is in the likeness of John de Rosen. This mural is painted on a false wall, set in toward the sanctuary about six or eight inches from the original wall, and is not a supporting wall. This was to avoid cracks, in the event the east wall ever suffered any damage. The red in the background was mixed in the choir room—again and again—until Mr. de Rosen was satisfied with the shade. Then he hired a commercial painter to do this menial work. Of course, he had by then finished all the other.

-Richard White

When Mr. de Rosen was painting the angel Jophiel, the Rector walked back and forth, past the work several times, and finally asked the artist, "Why are you spending so much time on the serpent?"

"Well," was the reply, "if evil is not pretty, why would anyone be tempted?"

-Sarah Loaring-Clark Flowers

The face of St. Priscilla in the Chapel of the Holy Spirit is that of Beth Rutland.

I have been told that the face of Jesus in the mural behind the Altar in the same chapel is that of Charles Bullard. The other figures are that of his assistant, Brown.

In the Lady Chapel, the face of the figure on the right as one faces the mural behind the Altar is that of Bill Burnett, and his hands are used in some images.

When he was painting and I would practice too much, he would complain that the walls vibrated and bothered him. A day or two later he would come looking for me, saying he was too lonely, and would I play the organ some.

While he was in Memphis, Mr. de Rosen bought a new car—a very sedate, blue coupe. When someone remarked that he looked just like a businessman, he took it back and exchanged it for a very snappy red roadster.

-Richard White

When the murals were finished, we wanted to have a service of dedication, with Mr. de Rosen as the speaker. He replied that, because he was a Roman Catholic, he could not speak at a worship service in another church. But he discussed the matter with his priest, and we worked it out. We had a service of Evening Prayer on a Sunday afternoon, extinguished our candles ending our service, then he spoke about the murals.

-The Reverend Mr. Wallace Pennepacker

The Rev. Mr. Wallace Pennepacker remembers seeing The Rev. Mr. Loaring-Clark sitting in the back of the church watching Mr. de Rosen finish the mural over the High Altar. It was virtually complete. The scaffolding was removed for the Rector's funeral two days later, February 23, 1952.

One of the first tasks The Rev. Mr. Pennepacker faced when he succeeded The Rev. Mr. Loaring-Clark was to work with Mr. de Rosen to decide what the subject matter of the remaining murals would be, and how they would be organized.

The next mural painted was Christ the Judge—painted as a memorial to The Rev. Mr. Loaring-Clark. Mr. de Rosen offered to do the work for whatever amount of money was given as memorials to the late Rector.

There had been no overall plan about the subject matter for the murals; perhaps they were begun without commitments for either the number or the memorials. The

The eight large murals were appraised . . . at a value of $98,000.

Rector and the artist discussed theology as it related to the Anglican tradition, deciding upon the theme and images to appear in each mural.

Sometimes parishioners would ask the Rector about the artist's working hours or anticipated completion date. But The Rev. Mr. Pennepacker believed that an artist could not work well under conditions of punching a time clock or being paid by the hour. Once the overall decisions were made, the artist was allowed to work out the paintings as he chose.

The murals were painted between the fall of 1949 and the spring of 1953, and cost $26,500. The eight large murals were appraised in 1976 by Michael Milkovich, then Director of The Dixon Gallery and Gardens, as having a value of $98,000.

In May 1957 David Fox Taylor submitted his thesis paper *Twentieth Century Church Decoration and the Contribution of John H. de Rosen* to the Department of Art and Archeology of Princeton University "in partial fulfillment of the requirements for the degree of Bachelor of Arts."

View from the Tower Room

When Bishop Quintard founded Episcopal Church-women in Tennessee more than 100 years ago, he set in motion an energy toward both specific needs of the church and outreach for local and foreign missions. The women at Calvary Episcopal Church had set an example for other new churches in the new Western District. Shortly after Calvary was organized in 1832, they assumed a role in preparing for holy days and ministering to the needy. Of the 10 original members who organized the church, six were women—although records found in more recent time suggest that one other woman and two men must have been among the organizers.

The Women of St. John's were organized early in the history of the Parish. Many records prior to the 1920s were lost, but minutes of the Women's Auxiliary predate The Rev. Mr. Loaring-Clark by more than a decade. Records for nearly a century show that they served dinners for the Vestry, gave luncheons for members of Women's Auxiliary, and honored the church school faculty with dinners.

During early years the men's groups were concerned with financial and maintenance problems, while the women could devote more time to missions.

They cared for altar linens for St. John's and for the Church Home. They took magazines, flowers, Bibles, and Christmas gifts to the Church Home, Crippled Children's Hospital, women at the penal farm, and to Mary Galloway Home—as these were established. They visited the sick. But the organization began as a mission study, with a separate group devoted to Altar Guild work. During the early years the men's groups were concerned with financial and

Sewanee Conference, Women of the Church, Libber Carey, Anne Connor, Celeste Vaiden

maintenance problems, while the women could devote more time to missions. As the Parish gained security, both local and foreign missions gained in priority.

The Rev. Mr. Loaring-Clark accentuated the Parish's mission as missionaries.

> We recognize, too, that we have a mission to heal the sick, minister to the broken-hearted, bind up the wounds of those whom life has hurt, and in so far as we can, feed the hungry. Around such an ideal the social service work of St. John's is built. We recognize that such work is but second best. The real task of the church is to create such a society, both economic and social, that these human tragedies will not occur. For the church, no less than medicine, has preventive work to do.
> *- Alfred Loaring-Clark, 1936*

At the Parish Meeting on January 14, 1936, Mr. Shuabel Beasley urged St. John's to take more interest in Boy Scouts work as a means to help the community. By

"Remember the starving children in Africa"

1943, Brownie Troop #84 thanked the Vestry for use of a church building in which to have meetings.

St. John's major mission effort was in sending two of their own to what was then called "Darkest Africa."

The slogan admonishing children to "Remember the starving children in Africa" seemed especially relevant at St. John's. Billy Rogers Beasley, son of Mr. and Mrs. Shubael Beasley, and his wife "Trink" left their comfortable Memphis situation to be missionaries in Liberia.

"Trink" was the former Marion Kathryn Goedjen of Green Bay, Wisconsin—called "Trinket" by her friends. They took Christianity, medicine, and the first Jeep to the mountains of Liberia, near the intersection of Sierra Leone, in 1951.

The mission of St. Joseph's Hospital, established by the Episcopal Order of the Holy Cross, had not had a doctor in over seven years. Dr. Beasley heard about it just as he was completing his internship at Charity Hospital in New Orleans.

Billy Rogers Beasley

At mid-20th century, Monrovia, the capital of Liberia, did not offer much more than Germantown—which was then farms and a few stores at Poplar and Germantown Road—but the interior was even more contrasting. The Beasleys reported that agriculture did not "even include a crude plow—only a hoe with a short handle; and there's no such thing as a cart with a wheel."

In October 1951 their destination was a four-day journey from the port in Sierra Leone—two days by the "Express" train, the next day by lorry, and the last day on foot. They made the rigorous journey with two toddlers

The Beasleys reported that agriculture did not "even include a crude plow—only a hoe with a short handle; and there's no such thing as a cart with a wheel."

aged one and two. Their third child, Battle, (now an Episcopal priest) was born in Africa.

Dear Family:

We arrived in Freetown at 6:00 a.m.; Father Parcell and the Bolahun Chief, Patrick Seafe, came out to the boat to meet us. Patrick was tall, with magnificent dignity. The beau ideal of a chief. . . . [Customs] managed to hold back the seed suitcase, for seeds cannot be brought into Sierra Leone. . . . Freetown itself is on hills, some as steep as San Francisco. Small, rugged hills. . . . Thousands of Mohammedans, with brilliantly embroidered fezzes and flowing robes. Two-thirds of the population carrying the loads on their heads. . . . The express train [from Freetown] was a narrow gauge that swayed like the old Peabody trolley used to do and averages 10 1/2 miles an hour. That was the express! . . .

[After the train for two long days, a lorry for an even longer day plus, on the fourth day, seventeen miles to the end of the road, they were met by the Bolahun carriers for the last eight hours. The last four hours were] straight up

You must know I was reduced to tears . . . from overwhelming humility and being so beautifully welcomed in such a Christian manner by such simple and honest people. . . .

and straight down. Sewanee Mountain, without stopping, for four hours! . . . A very fine avenue of cola trees led into the village of mud houses. We were surrounded by a huge throng, some playing harmonicas, some flutes, some singing, and all utterly joyful. Directly we went to the large church and straightway to the altar rail. Brother Sidney had preceded me into the church and was filling it with glorious organ music. A prayer of thanksgiving was said, and translated into Bandi; we were blessed, and all finally

---

Of Your Kindness, Please Share Our Prayers:

For blessing on the Surgical and Medical work of Dr. Beasley.

That we may raise up more Christian teachers to strengthen Kpandemai, Gondolahun and Vahun.

That the new staff and girls at Vezala may steadfastly witness for Christ.

That the newly baptised and confirmed may persevere.

In Past Year the Clinic has given 22,563 treatments to 2,257 persons, for Yaws, Malaria, Sleeping Sickness, and vaccinations.

sang a glorious doxology. You must know I was reduced to tears . . . from overwhelming humility and being so beautifully welcomed in such a Christian manner by such simple and honest people. . . . The house had been carefully cleaned, a garden planted around, flowers inside and out, beds were up, and after a brief supper we gratefully crawled under the nets.

—*Willie*

Oct. 21, 1951
Dear Family,
    . . . The house is mighty plain but will change. Covered with a corrugated iron roof, a large sign at the bottom of the path reads: Dr. W.B.R. Beasley, M.D. Living room has eight windows, is about 15 by 22. A porch will be built sometime. Kitchen is separate—a little thatched house on stilts. . . . The Staff consists of six Sisters, Fr. Parcell, Fr. Taylor (Dean Stewart's friend), Fr. DeCota,

". . .it does keep one busy."

a Canary Island Priest who has worked in Africa a number of years, Minty Simpson, Dr. Beasley. They have a boarding school for boys and one for girls, for primary school—quite remarkable. . . . In Church School . . . men sit on one side, women on the other . . . and stray dogs.

—*Trink*

Nov. 19
    . . . The hospital has increased in volume. At present, we are treating about 80 patients every Friday for sleeping sickness. We can see malaria in blood smear. So far about 10 lepers have appeared—all very advanced cases. We are in hopes of arranging a leper village in a month or so, to start treating them. If so, we shall use some of the

Gregg money for medicine. Financially the cost of dressers is about $70 per month for the hospital, and we expect a monthly order of penicillin and sulphur to run about $75. . . . Our hospital fees have brought in about $50 or $60 a week, so we hope to have some money left over for extra medicine and equipment. [In March, they wrote that everyone was required to pay, even if only one banana, with the fees primarily for surgery. The people in Bolahun paid at most $1, regardless of how large the surgery, and Christians were given a discount.] Hospital buildings—there is a brick dispensary about 40 by 25. There are three wards—one wooden with 12 beds, one semi-cement with metal roof, with 20 beds, and one pure native which is half women's ward with 8 or 10 beds and half cooking room to heat food and water.

—*W.B.R.B.*

Nov. 27
    The house: we have lived at Robinwood — Anne Hathaway — The Tenement — the Chicken Coop, and this — well, Bleak House would be fitting. Concrete square with a corrugated iron roof, for which I am duly thankful for no rats or snakes can bed down. This past week marks the completion of our Mary Martin shower — my face and feet can be seen from above and below the bamboo mat walls. . . . We have a staff or four or almost five, but with no running water and a well several hundred yards away; wood to be searched for and cut, for three meals as well as boiling drinking water, bath water, laundry water, baby bottles, etc.; lamps to be cleaned and filled, children to be watched, etc., it does keep one busy.

—*Love, Trinket*

Jan. 5, 1952

Christmas is over; the dressers have almost recovered from their three days of all day work and all night dancing . . . [We sorted] four bags of mail and packages; there are still seven bags at Bueda. Very grand, as we have really had no mail for three weeks. We have received the yeast, the filiforms, the *Illustrated London News* from Sister Eleanor (which has been passed on to the sisters who devour them even more eagerly than we), Mrs. Hazlehurst's eggs and *caviar*, detective stories, Dorothy Sayer carton of books, the developing tray and mosquito bombs. . . . we sit by the Coleman, wrapped in a marvelous gown of country cloth given me by a clan chief. That same chief has promised us 50 carriers for this next week, so we hope most of the stuff will get over from Bueda except the iceboxes, of course. It means the rest of the surgical equipment, including the primus stove, so no charcoal stove will be needed. . . . New tables are being built for the surgery and pharmacy and . . . we hope to begin surgery

In truth, Zacharias is the missionary to me. [This was a man that] was being trained as a Bandi Devil when the mission came.

this month. . . . I have pre-spent Tata's money on eye instruments, one of which I could not get here and so the head blacksmith, who is also a goldsmith, is making one for me.
—*Much love to all, Trink and Willie*

Wish you could have been here for the Christmas pageant. The audience was composed of several hundred school children (most of the children are boarders and return at the holiday from their own town — some several days' walk away), the townspeople, heathen from the countryside, three devils, the mission staff, and four English visitors. Two unrehearsed bits were the shepherds crooks—which were 15 feet in height and could only have been used to round up stray giraffe; the other, Salome whipped out a pocket knife, reached overhead, plucked an orange off a tree and peeled it for Herod, who juicily sucked it during his interview with the three wisemen.

[A letter in February told that Zacharias, the head Evangelist who had played Herod in the Christmas pageant was suddenly stricken with a form of cerebral malaria that] usually kills in 24 hours what was a healthy man. Zach had called his eldest son and had carefully explained certain people who had been especially kind to him and to whom his son should be helpful in every possible manner. He had sent word to Fr. that he wishes to make his confession. He prayed the utmost that God would look after and bless his family and . . . these prayers were devoid of any intercession for himself other than a reaffirmation of his trust in God. . . . In truth, Zacharias is the missionary to me. [This was a man that] was being trained as a Bandi Devil when the mission came.

Jan. 13

With a full moon once again, the evening dancing has been resumed and we can hear the drums and voices of neighboring villages late at night. The people have wedding feasts and dances and 'wake' feasts and dancing and on other full moon nights have dances just for pleasure. We walked over to a neighboring town to watch the dancing . . . not the fiendish tribal rite we had hoped to witness, but rather a version of the Big Apple which was so popular a decade ago. . . . Heavy mist shrouding the tops of palm trees, bodies swaying to the rhythm of the drums; thru a door partly open in a native hut could be seen several women sitting around a fire in the middle of the round mud house, the room filled with warm smoke. The walk home thru high elephant grass

"Willie"

and a swamp with the wind crackling the dry grass made the short outing seem quite exciting.

Jan. 27

We have had only a three-minute sprinkle in the last three months and it is now as hot and dry as a Memphis drought; instead of freezing under four blankets as we were three weeks ago, we now swelter under a single sheet.

Trink is to teach a 10th grade class in English and history. She would like very much to have the National Geographic maps. There are no maps for the school children. Her history course is to begin with Charlemagne.

—*Love, Trink and Willie*

In March 1952 the Beasleys and Fr. Parcell wrote to Mr. & Mrs. Shubael Beasley in Memphis about the need for transportation, requesting a Jeep. After much investigation, pricing, and correspondence, the Beasleys bought the Jeep with the help of many contributors from home.

Supplies and gifts from many people included medicine contributed by Grace-St. Luke's as well as St. John's.

They finally actually got the Jeep with the help of many natives who pushed, pulled, lifted, and built roads for the four days of tough travel. Mapping a circuitous route, they could drive the vehicle "from Sierra Leone up to French Guinea, take a fine road through part of the French [territory] country, approach Liberia from the top side, come down past a Swedish Pentecostal mission, and join a road being worked on that came within three miles of Bolahun." When the vehicle slithered into mud from planks laid to bridge a swampy fork of a river, the laborers lifted the 3,000 or more pounds of the loaded car to safety—although they were standing almost knee-deep in mud. "The Day the Jeep Arrived" was not the only event made possible by Memphis friends and relatives. Supplies and gifts from many people included medicine contributed by Grace-St. Luke's as well as St. John's.

One of the most practical gifts to the Beasleys came from Dr. Beasley's childhood friend, David Fox.

The Beasleys' cook needed teeth, and Dr. Beasley appealed to Dr. Fox because there were no dentists in the Bolahun vicinity. Dr. Beasley wrote a description of the problem to Dr. Fox, who sent detailed instructions and materials for making a plaster impression. Dr. Beasley made the cast and sent it to Dr. Fox, who sent back a set of teeth that fit the cook perfectly.

The Beasleys returned to Memphis in 1954, and Dr. Beasley went on staff at Methodist Hospital. The Men's Club invited Dr. Beasley to speak about the Holy Cross Mission in Liberia; a large crowd came to hear him.

Money from St. John's went to mission funds in Africa, India, Japan, Brazil, American Indian reservations, Orange Mound, Hawaii—primarily for education.

The Diocesan Convention in 1965, held at St. John's, voted to provide an airplane for the use of Bishop Brown in Liberia; the women of St. John's started the fund with a contribution of $100.

Yogyakarta, Indonesia

It's October, 1980 and I'm trying to make a tape for you about what I can remember of St. John's history. It is shamelessly woven with all kinds of family recollections.
–W.B.R.B

The Beasley family moved to Gwynne Road in 1927. They were members of St. Mary's Cathedral, changing to St. John's the following year. Dr. Beasley said that it was

"I can remember us driving in a model-T Ford along with the Farnsworths across the state, to climb the Sewanee mountain and spend two weeks there."

the result of several factors. "The Beasleys went to early Service, the Beasleys went to Sunday School, and the Beasleys went back to the 11 o'clock Service, so this meant three trips from the Cathedral to Gwynne Road on Sunday, which was a difficult and long haul."

In his reminiscences, Dr. Beasley told about the emphasis placed on religious education when he was a child at St. John's. During the 1930s the Beasley family attended the two weeks training for all the Sunday School teachers in the Diocese. "I can remember us driving in a model-T Ford along with the Farnsworths across the state, to climb the Sewanee mountain and spend two weeks there. I remember it so well because the model-T Ford boiled over before we got to the top."

His mother, Mrs. Shubael Beasley (Irene), was Superintendent of the Sunday School and set many requirements. Children memorized the catechism; learned to name the parts of the *Book of Common Prayer* and the contents of each, its origins and how to use the Prayer Book;

learned to recite the seasons of the liturgical year and what each season stood for; and had many more departmental and individual class requirements.

"Most outstanding about the Lenten choir was . . . Mr. Tib, who spoke to the choir on Tuesdays and Wednesdays. He would stand in the middle of the chancel step, put his watch on the chancel rail—his watch used to have a little gold basketball or football on it—and talk to us. He talked a great deal about missions, about Father Damien [Belgian missionary to lepers] and Dr. Schweitzer [Dr. Albert Schweitzer, authority on Bach and missionary to Africa who won the Nobel Peace Prize while the Beasleys were at the Bolahun mission]; he told us many hero stories [such as about] Sister Teresa. . . . This made a very significant impact on most everyone in the choir."

Dr. & Mrs. Shubael Beasley

August 2, 1950

My dear Penny:

An hour or so ago I said goodbye to you at the plane with some reluctance. It was a perfectly grand experience to have had the three days with you . . . .Whatever the leadership in St. John's has been during the past 20 years . . .I do know that we have grand, responsive, warmhearted and consecrated people . . . . [The committee] are unanimous in their hope that you will come to be our associate rector . . . . If you come to St. John's, the committee

"*. . . if you decide to come, it would be a very happy experience for the Loaring-Clarks and I hope for the Pennepackers . . .*"

does not wish to force you to live in the present associate rector's house, but is willing to make every reasonable effort to secure a house with three bedrooms. In the words of [the committee], "We certainly do not wish to lose Mr. Pennepacker solely because of one bedroom."

. . . if you decide to come, it would be a very happy experience for the Loaring-Clarks and I hope for the Pennepackers, if you all would come and stay with us before your furniture arrives and spend a few days looking over places to live. Clara and I would love that.

I tell you again as I have many times, that I think you would have a fine creative ministry in St. John's and that you and your family would have the love, respect and admiration of our congregation which every priest of the church surely wishes. Certainly if you come you will have my loyalty and support.

Yours in Christ,
Alfred Loaring-Clark

Less than two years later, at a called meeting, the Vestry made The Rev. Mr. Pennepacker acting Rector until such time as permanent arrangements were made. Then at a special Vestry meeting on March 12, 1952, it was unanimously approved to call The Rev. Mr. Wallace M. Pennepacker to succeed the late Rev. Mr. Alfred Loaring-Clark as Rector.

He served the Parish as Rector until his retirement nearly 31 years later.

Affectionately known as "Penny" to Parish and friends, The Rev. Mr. Pennepacker came to St. John's from Ho-Ho-Kus, New Jersey, after meeting The Rev. Mr.

He had meant to be an educator, and, as a priest, carried forth that calling.

Loaring-Clark one summer at Sewanee. He had meant to be an educator, and, as a priest, carried forth that calling.

October 24, 1950

Rev. Wallace M. Pennepacker
St. John's Church
Central & Greer
Memphis 11, Tenn.

Dear Mr. Pennepacker:

Thanks for your letter of the 20th and
the enclosed letter dimissory which I am
happily accepting today. I am notifying
Bishop Washburn accordingly.

We are delighted to have you with us in
Tennessee and hope and believe that you will
be happy in our diocesan fellowship.

With all good wishes,

Faithfully yours,

E. P. Dandridge

epd/ss

Born and educated in Philadelphia, Wallace Pennepacker began working toward a Master of Arts in Education at the University of Pennsylvania. He detoured from studies to teach at The Gilman School for a year, and returned to divinity school instead of his previous graduate program. After graduation from Philadelphia Divinity School (now the Episcopal Divinity School in Cambridge, Massachusetts following a merger), he was Assistant Rector at two churches before becoming Rector at the New Jersey church.

He had been Rector at the church in Ho-Ho-Kus for five years when a professor asked him to fill in as teacher for a summer course at Sewanee. Among the people he met there was Alfred Loaring-Clark.

"When 'Tib' contacted me about being the Assistant Rector at St. John's," he recalls, "I thought of all the people I had met at Sewanee, thought about how I had considered relocating to that part of the country, and how nice it sounded. But after being assistant in two churches, I had had my own church for five years, and was not sure I

Basketball team, 1959

could be called as Rector. But I certainly did not expect to again have my own church so soon."

The first thing he did was to ask the Vestry for a Director of Christian Education rather than an Associate Rector.

On Trinity Sunday the next year, he preached that:

"We are proclaiming, on this Sunday each year, that all that God was and is to people, all that He has done and is doing, hangs together. It is all a deliberate design on His part.

We reflect this unity of purpose and plan in our own lives by . . . a rebirth of the spirit, a change of attitude."

With a small staff and a confirmed commitment to organization, he spent most of his time on church business. He served as a member of the Bishop and Council of the Episcopal Diocese of Tennessee, on Memphis Ministerial Council (elected President in 1961), Memphis Council on Alcoholism, one of six examining chaplains for the Episcopal Diocese of Tennessee for those to be ordained,

". . . It is all a deliberate design on His part."

a member of the Diocese Department of Church Education, and the Cluster of Churches. Occasionally, though, he was able to indulge his love for fishing when a parishioner invited him. He enjoys telling about the time that he and Fritz Schas had a paddler at Menasha who knew the right spots and they piled the boat with about 100 fish. It was a rare respite.

His wife, Frances, was the community spirit, active in catalytic health and welfare organizations. Born Frances Roome, in Washington, D.C., she graduated from Temple

wanted to be assistant, even in a larger church." The Rev. Mr. Loaring-Clark asked him to just come for a visit, no hard feelings if it didn't seem right to accept. And The Rev. Mr. Pennepacker visited.

"St. John's was a growing church and a wonderful place," he says. "When 'Tib' explained the need for a Christian Education leader who wanted to work with the young people, I felt that it was the right place for me. So my wife, Frances, our two little daughters, Carol and Jane, and I moved to Memphis. We were here for just 16 months before 'Tib' died. In those days it was allowed that an assistant

University. She helped establish the Memphis Literary Council and Tennessee Chapter of Cystic Fibrosis Foundation. She served on many health and welfare boards such as Memphis Health and Welfare Planning Council, United Way of Greater Memphis, Foundation for World Literacy, Orange Mound Day Nursery, Volunteer Service Bureau, and United Church Women. Prior to her death in 1989 she was organizing and compiling records for a history of St. John's.

The Rev. Mr. Pennepacker—scholar, educator, organizer—spent hours in preparation for each service, and for the years when there was no assistant, he conducted four services each Sunday.

One of his first duties was to manage the completion of the new church. In February 1953, the Vestry voted to sell blocks of marble for the floor, and mailed an appeal to the parishioners to buy the blocks at three dollars each. By June, the sales amounted to over $5,000, with 50 blocks donated by the Church School. It was still not quite enough to lay all the marble, and the gap was filled with

. . . the Vestry voted to sell blocks of marble for the floor . . .at three dollars each.

donations from Russell Gregg, Jim Robinson, and Mr. and Mrs. Jules Rozier. The Rev. Mr. Pennepacker and the Vestry held meetings with the architect, Mr. Lucian Dent, and finalized the plans for the interior.

Costs for everything rose and the church had extraordinary expenses in 1953, leaving a deficit of $1,727.07. The pledge campaign was $9,331.80 short, making it necessary to cut the budget items for an associate rector and several church planning items.

With a growing church school and diminished staff, the search for a Director of Christian Education accelerated. Miss Katherine Sensabaugh was hired in September 1952, but resigned after only two months, due to ill health.

"Elinor, if you know Jesus Christ and your Bible, that's enough."

The search began again. In January 1953 the Vestry approved hiring Miss Erna Blaydow from All Saints in Worchester, Massachusetts. The teaching ministry grew.

Mrs. John Austin, Jr. (Susan Fulmer) recalls that her mother, Mrs. John Fulmer, took Miss Blaydow to lunch each Friday. During a period when Mrs. Fulmer couldn't keep the commitment, she asked Susan to fill in. "She was an incredible person," Susan remembers, "and the best read person I've ever met. She talked about art, history, philosophy, literature—and she loved music."

Elinor Turner went to Miss Blaydow's classes regularly, both the teacher training and Wednesday Bible classes. In her reminiscences, Mrs. Turner relates that, "I remember once saying to her, 'Oh, how I wish I had studied Plato, Aristotle, Socrates, and the other great philosophers,' many of whom she would quote. Her answer was, 'Elinor, if you know Jesus Christ and your Bible, that's enough.'"

With all the changes at St. John's, the Vestry noted that the Parish had a 75-year history that needed recording. It was recommended that Mr. Enoch Mitchell be asked to be parish historian, so there would always be records available. Dr. Mitchell, first Chairman of the Department of History at (then) Memphis State Teachers' College, died in 1965. He was eulogized by MSU President Cecil C. Humphreys as "one of the South's best known historians." The connection with St. John's continues, with Parishioners such as Dr. William R. Gillaspie, Dr. James Chumney, and Dr. William Marty.

A substantial gift of $7,000 in June 1954 was to be used at the Vestry's discretion, and that made possible completion of plastering and wainscoting in the church proper. When Shubael Beasley died that fall, the Vestry established as a memorial to him a new teaching classroom for the church school. At the request of the Beasley Family, money given as memorials for Mr. Beasley was used to establish this new teaching laboratory. Space on the second floor of the East (Church School) Building was petitioned into small class rooms for the Church School. (The area is presently used for church offices.)

The turmoil of the 20th Century did not abate during the second half. Pork Chop Hill. Red baiting. The McCarthy Hearings and black listing. Television. Bay of Pigs. The moon landing. Viet Cong. Flower Power. Assassination. "God is Dead." Secularism. Martin Luther King. Revisions of the Bible, prayer book, hymnal. The sexual revolution. Roe v. Wade. Two-income families. Civil Rights. Cold War. AIDS.

The decade of the 1950s—called "the Last Age of Innocence"—moved swiftly toward the storms of change. As hostilities mushroomed into a cloud over the future, atrocities were mirrored in the newly accessible television screen.

Publications in 1948 and 1953 of Dr. Alfred Charles Kinsey's studies of human sexuality are said to have been

"Penny" with Mr. and Mrs. Dick Walker. "Installation of the French brass bell, cast in 1960, was delayed until instructions in English could be provided to the electrician." -Richard White

the catalyst for the sexual revolution, which also revolutionized and polarized doctrinal tenets of mainstream conservative as well as more liberal congregations. It took by surprise clergy and lay leaders struggling to redefine responsibilities of the church toward parishioners and community during the social upheaval of the 1960s. Mr. Pennepacker recalls that many weeks he was immersed in counseling his parishioners about topics that had previously not been problems brought on such a scale to a rector.

Mr. Pennepacker says that he has always believed in reasonableness, not dogmatics; in dialogue, which is educational, not just the monologue of a sermon. Parishioners remember him as a nurturing, caring person who could be counted on in times of personal crisis. In describing his methods, one parishioner relates that her family once had a crisis when their daughter refused to go to school. She called Mr. Pennepacker in distress. When he arrived at their house, he said that he wanted to talk with only the daughter, and the two of them shut the door of the room while they talked. They later emerged smiling,

. . . a nurturing, caring person who could be counted on in times of personal crisis.

and Mr. Pennepacker related "our decision" to the parents. The mother marveled that he always credited the other person with arriving at the right decision.

In April 1954, the Bishop suggested that St. John's give $1,000 per year to St. Edward's, a Diocesan mission, and use their deacon as an assistant at St. John's. Jack Bowling was introduced to the Vestry on July 14, as a help to Mr. Pennepacker.

Jane and Carol Pennepacker entertained Christine Badham of England, at the "Old Rectory," 1958

In 1955 The Rev. Mr. Pennepacker received a letter from the National Episcopal Church in New York asking if he would go to St. Augustin's the next year for a special program. The national church also wrote to Bishop Theodore Nott Barth to ask for Diocesan support for Mr. Pennepacker. The special assignment was a 10-month program at the Central College of the Anglican Community in Oxford, with the purpose of bringing together various members of the Anglican Community from throughout the world. With study and interaction, the group would learn of other, different parishes, bridging chasms of national and cultural differences.

St. John's gave him 10 months leave of absence, continuing his salary, and the Pennepackers went to England from September 1956 to July 1957.

Every Tuesday was a Common Room meeting, with lectures by such as the Archbishop of Canterbury. One sidelight of the stay was an invitation from the Dean of Canterbury Cathedral to tea at the Deanery. The Dean's daughter and the Pennepackers' daughters were at the same school, resulting in the invitation when the Dean learned that The Rev. Mr. Pennepacker was among attendees of the special program.

Archbishop Hewlett Johnson invited all four Pennepackers to tea, and the visit extended for hours. He invited The Rev. Mr. Pennepacker to preach at the Cathedral, but the Pennepackers were leaving for home and he could not accept the invitation.

The Rev. Mr. Arthur W. Fippinger came as Associate Rector in January 1956. Dorothy Houston Pennepacker (whose first memories of St. John's were from visits there with her aunt and uncle, Beth and Kimbrough Rutland) recalls that Mr. Fippinger hired her as church secretary during the time The Rev. Mr. Pennepacker was studying in England. When the Fippingers had a baby, Dorothy and Marion Reece, who was also on the staff, tied a pink bow around one of the trees on the Greer side of the church to tell the news, since there had been so much interest shown by the whole parish family.

In 1957 contributions were over $100,000. The Cloister Garden was designed in 1957, planned for 1958.

Membership at the beginning of 1958 was 1,137. New buildings were occupied, activities expanded, and the Parish grew. Boy Scout Troop #42 was sponsored by St. John's. The Parish bought a new rectory on Burgundy in 1959.

Cloister Garden

The Rev. Mr. Fippinger left in 1958 for St. George's in Nashville. The Rev. Mr. Gordon Bernard, who had 14 years experience in teaching, came with his wife and two little daughters to be Assistant Rector. He was to be ordained to the priesthood the next year.

When The Rev. Mr. Pennepacker resigned in 1983, after 31 years as Rector, the Vestry and Parish expressed a sense of loss. Despite his giving six months' notice, St. John's was without a rector for almost a year.

Ordination of Gordon Bernard,
March 16, 1960

His retirement from St. John's was not retirement from the ministry. He has responded to churches in need across the Diocese, preaching at Grace-St. Luke's, St. Phillip's Davieshire, All Saints, and has served as Canon to the Bishop.

In 1990, Mr. Pennepacker married Dorothy (Dottie) Gillespie, who also had been widowed for a number of years. Dottie served on the Altar Guild for most of her adult life and was Chairman for 11 years. She has fulfilled many responsibilities on the Altar Guild and is especially noted for flower arranging. Mr. Pennepacker's family also includes his daughter Jane Pienaar, her sons Bryan Lawton (the eldest grandson) and David; his daughter and son-in-law, Carol and Richard Walker, and their children Richard III and Carol. Dottie's children and grandchildren are Paul Trowbridge Gillespie, Jr. and Elizabeth (Johnston), Paul III, Stuart, and John; and Gaye and Haywood Henderson, Jr., Whitney, Dorothy, and Grace.

St. John's Episcopal Church
Central and Greer
Memphis, Tennessee 38111

May 19, 1983

The Rev. Wallace M. Pennepacker
St. John's Episcopal Church
32 South Greer
Memphis, Tennessee   38111

Dear Penny:

When your letter of resignation was read to the Vestry, it was accepted with the very deepest regret.

Everyone present welcomed the opportunities that this will open for you, and we hope your retirement will be filled with continued good health and many interesting and enjoyable activities. Because of your experience, excellent judgment and wisdom, your advice and help will always be sought by individuals as well as by the Church.

Upon learning of your decision, the reaction of the Vestry was, of course, one of great disappointment. We remembered the guidance, love and spiritual leadership that you have given us over the years. You have seen many grow up, helped with countless troubles and problems, and led us to a better understanding of what it means to be a Christian.

You will be missed terribly by everyone at St. John's. We offer our very best wishes to you and Frances for the years ahead.

Sincerely,

Seldon Murray, Senior Warden
The Vestry of St. John's Episcopal Church

On December 7, 1979, St. John's purchased a cemetery that had been established at the northeast corner of Central Avenue and Buntyn Street in the late 1870s.

Founded by Ridge High Baptist Church, later named Central Avenue Baptist Church, the small cemetery held identifiable markers of burials between 1877 and 1938. The earliest burial marker showed that William Lee Lowery, eight-year-old son of W. B. and S. E. Lowery, died on September 12, 1877. The latest tombstone date in 1938 was for Hannah J. Prescott, wife of James A. Prescott.

The historian for the little Baptist church recorded that the fearful yellow fever epidemics of the 1870s did not claim a single member of the church, but that "one . . . ex-member died."

The cemetery was owned by Ridgeway Baptist Church, which had inherited it through a gift from the

. . . the cemetery was a piece of history not quite fitted into the landscape of expansion until St. John's returned it to the status of a beautiful park.

family of Confederate veteran James Prescott to what was then Ridge High Baptist Church at Central and Buntyn. The name of the church changed when the location changed.

During the 40 years between the last burial and purchase of the cemetery by St. John's, commuters down Central Avenue and newcomers to town often asked about the little burial ground on the corner of Central and Lafayette. Although neglected except for occasional cleaning and mowing by volunteers and Boy Scouts, the cemetery was a piece of history not quite fitted into the landscape of expansion until St. John's returned it to the status of a beautiful park.

James D. Robinson

In 1979, Mr. James D. Robinson offered to the Vestry that he would provide cash gifts in sufficient amounts to purchase the cemetery property and to provide for necessary repairs and maintenance. His only requirement was that the amount be considered sufficient by the Vestry, and that he be provided with a double crypt personal plot.

From 1979 to 1982, contributions from Mr. Robinson totaled $450,000.

The cemetery was purchased for $10,117.50. The Rev. Mr. Wallace Pennepacker, Rector of St. John's, announced that the church would spend between $100,000 and

During the years before St. John's purchase, the corner often looked neglected.

$200,000 to redevelop the cemetery. Three phases of planned redevelopment included building a brick and wrought iron fence to enclose the property, with a gate opening onto Lafayette. In 1981-82 St. John's completely restored the beautiful grounds filled with towering oaks, built a brick wall and wrought iron fence around the entire cemetery, constructed a wrought iron gazebo on the grounds, and cleaned and re-set those markers that required attention. By mid-1983 most renovation was completed, costing in excess of $400,000. A permanent trust, under direction of the Vestry, governs the fund and staff, which are entirely separate from the church. The trust was established to manage the fund and to assure perpetual care. At the 25th anniversary, in 2007, the property reverts to St. John's rather than being a separate trust.

The cemetery had been marked by periods of neglect, then recognition. The cemetery's administrators considered moving the interred to Memorial Park, but law requires approval of every living relative before such a move, and the plan was abandoned. In 1940, the Buntyn City Beautiful Club renovated the cemetery, then called "the old Baptist Cemetery." In 1970, the Texas State Historical Survey Committee placed a marker on the grave of Jacob Covington (1838-1910), a Civil War veteran who in 1876 became the first district clerk in Camp County, Texas. During the years before St. John's purchase, the corner often looked neglected.

Originally, 775 burial spaces were marked off, initially to parishioners of St. John's and their immediate families. Some members expressed interest in underground crypts.

In 1984, Memphis Heritage, Inc. awarded its first Anona Stoner memorial to St. John's Episcopal Cemetery. The award was established by the Board of Directors to honor the memory of the long-time president of the Citizens to Preserve Overton Park. Its purpose was "to recognize outstanding efforts in the preservation and enhancement of the natural urban environment."

The cemetery was one of six architectural projects honored in ceremonies held jointly by Memphis Landmarks Commission and Memphis Heritage. In addition to the cemetery, architectural preservation projects cited were The Orpheum, the Porter Building, the Old Daisy Theater, One Union Place, and the Annesdale-Snowden Historic District.

There have been 76 burials since St. John's re-opened the churchyard in 1982.

James Robinson's tombstone weathered for many years, in Forest Hill Cemetery Midtown for 18 years

St. John's Episcopal Cemetery

before being moved to the location near his church. His plot is just inside the fence, in sight of the sixth green of the Memphis Country Club golf course. He meant it to be visible to his golf buddies every weekend. Mr. Robinson

"Old Robby, renowned golfer and bridge player. Tone bidder and oral specialist, who dealt. What's the score? Don't think—That's a funny thing—Review the bidding—The hell with it!"

loved to tell that his grandfather—the Confederate general from whom his middle name, Dinkins, came—prepared his tombstone 25 years before his death, and he followed in the tradition. "Old Robby, renowned golfer and bridge player. Tone bidder and oral specialist, who dealt. What's the score? Don't think—That's a funny thing—Review the bidding—The hell with it!"

After more than four decades of neglect, the 123-year-old cemetery looks respected again.

From 1982-1987 there were 24 burials; 64 plots and 18 niches were sold. Sales accelerated in 1995, with 37 lots and 7 niches sold. Lots are available to any Episcopalians and their families, not just to members of St. John's.

Mimi Mallory, first administrator of the cemetery

St. John's Episcopal Parish has a record of mission work and outreach before the Parish advanced beyond mission stage for the second time. Minutes from the St. John's Branch of the Women's Auxiliary meeting in December 1916 tell of sending one dollar in response to an appeal from The Rev. Mr. W. A. Cash in Lake Andes, South Dakota, who requested help in building an Episcopal church there. That money was the sum collected at the first meeting, held on October 19. There were five

> *. . . a substantial part of the money going to the girls who had been released from the penal farm to help them to get re-established.*

people in attendance: Mrs. C. E. Coe, President; Mrs. Palmer Farnsworth, Mrs. Kate Phillips, Miss Anna P. Phillips, and Mr. Knoft, who "opened and closed the meeting with devotional services." Mrs. Grant Knoft, Secretary, was absent. A letter from "Mrs. Loaring-Clark of Chattanooga" was read, and a response sent to her requesting suggestions for a book on mission study and some additional copies of the Order for Opening Services.

April 7, 1943 - Vestry Minutes
It was agreed that $35 be turned over each month to the ladies of the church for social service work as

they had many calls for rent and etc., a substantial part of the money going to the girls who had been released from the penal farm to help them to get re-established.

A January 1936 report told of a membership increase to 25 members for the Episcopal Student Club, also known as Unit #1, located at State Teacher's College (now University of Memphis). The club was sponsored by St. John's.

In 1949, during the Berlin Airlift, the Church School collected toys and clothing for the thousands of refugee children who flocked to Bavaria in the American Zone. They sent 16 boxes, weighing a total of 301 pounds, to distribute to some of the 25,000 children in displaced persons camps.

In a prophetic sermon in 1938, the Rev. Mr. Loaring-Clark said:

> Surely God wills unity where we now have strife— between capital and labor, between race and race, between nation and nation. The Christian Church, broken into fragments, must somehow and in God's own time be reconciled within itself.

Meade Nichol told that during the worst of the Depression, the Women's Auxiliary went to John Gaston

Hospital to take home premature babies who had to be left there. Their mothers had no means of transportation and no money to hire a taxi. The women of St. John's picked up the mothers, one at a time, took them to the hospital where they were instructed in the care and feeding of their babies, then took them home. They were given milk by the Cynthia Milk Fund. For a year, women from St. John's took food or whatever was needed to the mothers every week. Pat Saunders got jobs for many of them.

The weekly meetings and rehabilitation assistance

No longer was the mission field distant Africa; it was neighboring Orange Mound.

for women prisoners at the Penal Farm quietly set the pace for social activism decades before it became headlines. Such outreach programs characterize each report of every group in St. John's Parish, throughout the written records that are preserved. Mission reports talked about foreign missions; community outreach was written about as if an integral part of the church's mission. As the decade of the 1960s erupted from chaos to chaos, mission efforts changed from telescopic to microscopic. No longer was the mission field distant Africa; it was neighboring Orange Mound.

St. John's, however, had seen the want in nearby mission fields since Civil War days, working to establish an orphanage then. The Orange Mound Day Nursery was started by Mrs. Shubael Beasley in the early 1940s, just when the support for African missions was also commited and continuing. Every organization in the Parish looked for outreach avenues that would extend the faith legacy beyond geographic and membership bounds.

In the summer of 1960, about 20 EYC members from the diocese went to Mexico on a church service project. It was under the joint sponsorship of the Division of Youth of the Episcopal Diocese of Tennessee, the Missionary District of Mexico, and the summer service projects committee of the Episcopal Church's National Council. The Rev. Mr. David Jones from Christ Church in Whitehaven led the group, accompanied by one of his parishioners, Mr. Phillips, who drove the bus. It was an old school bus painted green that the group dubbed "El Perro Verde" (the green dog).

The group stayed in homes of Episcopalians for the two nights between Memphis and the border. Once they reached Mexico, the bus broke down frequently, causing headaches for the leaders but making an adventure for the young people.

Carolyn Forsythe recalls that they lived in a little town a few hours from Mexico City. The town had two Episcopal boarding schools, one for girls and one for boys.

"always an adventure, since our bus could be counted on to break down"

With the help of a Mexican named Ricky who interpreted for them, the enthusiastic group toured the area on weekends, "always an adventure, since our bus could be counted on to break down," recalls Carolyn. Whether or not they accomplished as much painting and roof repairing for the schools as they had hoped, the group did teach Vacation Bible School and enjoyed countless adventures. So much so that Carolyn Forsythe majored in Spanish at Purdue.

Orange Mound Day Nursery

The work of spreading the Gospel at home intensified when Otey Chapel Mission was assigned to St. John's as Parish Mission by the Department of Missions of the Diocese of Tennessee.

Terminology throughout the decade changed forever the vocabulary or brought stronger impact to words like civil rights, assassination, sit-in, march, busing, Flower Power, Vietnam, drugs, immigrants, Free Love, divorce, daycare, pop psychology, feminist, demonstration, Kent State.

In a 1962 sermon entitled "A Christian's Responsibility to the United Nations," The Rev. Mr. Pennepacker said, "100,000 Cuban refugees in Miami . . . [have] not enough food, clothing, shelter, jobs." The Episcopal Church had set up a center in Miami and donations were

"The idea of the framers of our Constitution was not freedom FROM religion, but freedom OF religion."

accepted at St. John's for Cuban refugee relief.

The U.S. Supreme Court ruled in June 1962 that it is unconstitutional to have prayers in public schools. As retiring president of the Memphis Ministers Association, The Rev. Mr. Pennepacker was interviewed by *Memphis Press-Scimitar*, and he disagreed with the ruling:

"Without SOME religious framework I don't believe there would even be a Constitution. . . . The idea of the framers of our Constitution was not freedom FROM religion, but freedom OF religion."

In May 1963, The Rev. Mr. Carter J. Gregory, a native of New York but then serving a church in Racine, Wisconsin, came to St. John's as Curate. He held a degree in philosophy and sociology from Hunter College, attended Philadelphia Divinity School, and received a degree in theology from the Nashotah House Seminary at Nashotah, Wisconsin.

The Anglican Congress of 1963 and General Convention of 1964 focused on concern for fellow Christians around the globe. Episcopalians were encouraged to study the document "Mutual Responsibility and Interdependence," advocating that Christians give an equal amount to others as spent on self.

In 1964, The Rev. Mr. George M. M. Thomson came from Edinburgh. He had traveled from New Orleans to Memphis the previous year and stopped off. While visiting with Mr. Pennepacker, he said that churches were better attended in the U.S. than in England.

The Rev. Mr. George M.M. Thomson

From 1964 to 1967 the church operated with a deficit budget. It was finally reduced to $431.73 in 1967. But the financial crunch and the many problems in 1965 fostered the Parish Planning Retreat and changes in programs.

The years 1966-67 were unusual for the EYC. They tried many new ideas.

At Annual Meeting in 1969 they auctioned off various services to raise money for a portable stage. Cost: $600. Raised: $489.16. The youth groups, both junior and senior high, have varied activities and studies to accommodate trends and to interest members during different trends. In the 1930s, for example, girls from the senior department of the Church School assisted in serving refreshments at the Women's Auxiliary annual garden party. Youth

EYC dinner preparation, 1959

groups have entertained at a costume party—with bunco and dancing; sponsored carnivals; produced plays and musicals; studied Russian; played basketball; organized dances, hayrides, and swimming parties; watched and discussed current movies (such as Corrie Ten Boom's *The Hiding Place* in 1975). They have been Teenager of the

Like all mainstream Protestant churches, St. John's struggled through the 1960s to redefine the role of the church in modern life

Week, science fair winners, newspaper editors, and Aquabelles (in the 1959 water ballet at Chickasaw Country Club).

The Men's Club planned more serious, formal programs, such as studying the "place of church and religion in modern living." They voted to recruit younger members, including college and pre-college age men, electing two college students to the board.

Like all mainstream Protestant churches, St. John's struggled through the 1960s to redefine the role of the church in modern life, and relevance of teaching forms. They tried new forms of worship, new literature, new liturgy as proposed by the national Episcopal Church.

There were 1,228 members in good standing in 1965; the deficit grew each year to $8,382.00 in 1965. The Men's Club began to have an annual Ladies Night. Mrs. Thomas (Martha) Lynch was hired as housekeeper. Indie Cockerham designed and initiated a project to sew vestments. She organized 15 women to meet twice weekly for the project.

It was an era when denominations tried to understand other denominations. The ecumenical movement began, as people of faith united to reach out to those in need, either physically or emotionally. In conjunction with other Midtown churches, St. John's sponsored the Half and Half Coffee House. Initiated by Dr. John William Aldridge, an assistant minister at Idlewild Presbyterian Church, sponsorship grew to include nine churches. The meeting place for young adults and "drop-outs" lasted from 1967 to 1974. While many conservative church members viewed such alternative outreach as unworthy of church sponsorship, the resultant agencies provided a safety net for many young people with drug problems or who ran away from home. Memphis House, drug abuse center, and the Runaway House (which grew into Family Link) were outgrowths of the Half and Half.

The Rev. Mr. George Thomson left in 1966 to become Curate at the Church of the Advent in Boston. In 1967, the

St. John's basketball team, Tom Lee-coach

Parish began a study to determine communicants' needs.

Mission work progressed, and the Otey Chapel Sunday School building was erected in 1968.

At the Annual Meeting, Richard Rodenbaugh reported on the sports program and said that St. John's "needs a recreation center."

Race relations in the city were more bifurcated than before, and religious leaders, both clergy and laity, worked at resolution.

Tensions mounted in Memphis throughout the later 1960s, culminating in the sanitation workers' strike and assassination of Dr. Martin Luther King on April 4, 1968. Race relations in the city were more bifurcated than before, and religious leaders, both clergy and laity, worked at resolution. Through the ecumenical efforts, the previously individual outreach programs grew into the clothes closet projects and lunch programs that became first Funds for Needy School Children, then matured into Metropolitan Interfaith Association (MIFA).

Many of the formerly dependable parishioners had second homes, and on weekends worshipped God in nature, not in church. Attendance and giving trends rollercoastered through the decade. Usually when an urgent appeal went out, the Parish responded with contributions. But the unrest of the era, the controversy with the National Council of Churches, the vision of "neighbor," and the changing familial patterns created unpredictable problems for the Rector and Vestry.

Three decades later, neoconservative sociologists such as historian Gertrude Himmelfarb would equate the counterculture of the 1960s with the proliferating social problems as the century ended. That society holds no strict sense of right and wrong, no clear sense of family and religious values, and has created a new vocabulary of rhetoric that removes responsibility from behavior is equated by Dr. Himmelfarb with the decline in societal morality.

As the Church United focused outward, bonds of faith loosened. Membership and contributions dropped. Dissension often created an amoeboe-like shifting of congregations moving, seeking. Writers have called the Baby Boomer generation the most questing group in recorded history. It is also the group that provides leadership for "re-engineering" parish traditions.

At the end of the decade the number of members in good standing was approximately the same as it had been 20 years previously—1,102. The annual budget was three times as large as in 1950, partially due to the changed value of the dollar and partly a true increase.

The Flower Children of the decade changed the way the Church viewed its responsibility to parishioners and community.

ANDERSON, CLAYTON & CO.
(INCORPORATED)

PO BOX 117
MEMPHIS 1, TENN.

June 24, 1965

The Rev. Wallace M. Pennepacker, Rector
St. John's Episcopal Church
322 South Greer Street
Memphis, Tennessee

Dear Rev. Mr. Pennepacker:

This will confirm the commitment I made with you today in reference to completing the cloister at St. John's Church during the calendar year 1965.

I hereby agree to donate sufficient money up to $30,000.00 for this purpose, payable as the work progresses and as the voucher's for labor and material are approved by you.

This letter when approved by you constitutes a contract between me and St. John's Episcopal Church covering the project described above.

Yours very truly,

Russell C. Gregg

RCG:mwc

The above letter constitutes the agreement between Russell C. Gregg and St. John's Episcopal Church of Memphis, Tennessee, made this 24th day of June, 1965.

The Rev. Wallace Pennepacker, Rector

COPY

omented in the suspicion of the late 1950s, simmered in decades of controversy, late 20th century people perceived shifting alliances. The mobile society was no longer loyal to business, church, or groups as "mine." Existentialistic ties to only the present loosened time-honored loyalty. Membership and stewardship suffered.

St. John's had 1,170 members in good standing at the end of 1969, and a deficit of $7,310.33, despite a balance of $3,290.85 carried forward from the 1968 budget. The staff was reorganized; The Rev. Mr. Frank T. Donelson, Jr. was

Break-ins and rising insurance rates mandated the change.

ordained Deacon, and—dictated by a changing society—the church was locked when not in use, beginning in the early 1970s. Break-ins and rising insurance rates mandated the change.

Perhaps most revealing of the differences between joy and duty is the E.Y.C. report at Annual Meeting on January 25, 1970.

"The programs [for 1969] consisted of a lecture on drug abuse, a program on alcoholism, a film on the making and dropping of the atom bomb, and a talk on communism and facism."

W. Harwell Allen, Jr., Senior Warden, at annual meeting in January 1970 said that, "The decade of the 1960s just ended has been almost the equivalent of the total second half of the 19th century in terms of technological and economic advances and the new problems, particularly in the field of human relations, which develop with such a high growth rate, have become almost overwhelming."

The 1970s decade began with reports at the Annual Parish Meeting of declining attendance and a deficit. The

"The decade of the 1960s just ended has been almost the equivalent of the total second half of the 19th century in terms of technological and economic advances and the new problems. . ."

following year also showed a deficit, although smaller. For both years the problem arose from unpaid pledges that had been factored into the budget. A new Charter and Bylaws for the Parish were presented at the 1971 gathering, but Dr. Duane Carr requested that adoption be postponed until everyone interested had an opportunity to read the documents.

Vestry and staff were reorganized in 1969-70, with the formation of committees composed of Vestry, staff, parishioners, and clergy, as needed. A new visitation program called "SEOPP" (acrynom for "St. John's Expansion of Parish Power"), was instigated in 1970, with the mission of providing feedback to the clergy and Vestry and of increasing church attendance and involvement.

The assessment of James C. Rainer, III, Senior Warden, was that "Nineteen Seventy was a very challenging year to the Episcopal Church in general, and to St. John's

"Nineteen Seventy was a very challenging year to the Episcopal Church in general, and to St. John's in particular.

in particular. I ended the year with the feeling that the change and reconciliation that took place in both the National Church and the local parish did so without destroying the effectiveness of either." There were 1,102 members in good standing, a budget of $150,665.36, and $157,969.25 spent, plus $537.50 deficit carried forward.

The Otey Chapel mission had a Wurlitzer electronic-reed organ—new to them— and nine new communicants from the confirmation class. The budget was $17,600, and was met by the help of a few extra fund-raising projects such as a mailing of 40,000 for Phi Mu National Sorority, which netted $500. Richard C. Maddock, Vicar of Otey Chapel, reported that "Our financial picture is still grim" to start 1970. One proposed solution was a return to part-time ministry.

The demise of the Men's Club in 1970 was particularly distressing, said James C. Rainer, III, Senior Warden, to the Annual Parish Meeting. The St. John's Men's Club started in 1946, meeting in Wager Hall at the Semmes and Spottswood location. Usually, The Rev. Mr. Loaring-Clark

was speaker during the early years of the group. It began with 15 to 20 men in attendance, and the Women's Auxiliary served dinner for the group. Attendance rose to about 100-125 during the years between 1948 and 1960. The Men's Club was for many years the maintenance group for the church. The members and anyone they could encourage to volunteer met to do repairs, paint, rake leaves, and generally assume responsibility for renovation and repairs.

The General Convention of Episcopal Churches in Houston in 1970 committed all Episcopalians to some kind of "Trial" for 1970-73. The Rev. Mr. Pennepacker told the Parish meeting in 1971 that the commitment of "Our 'Trial Services' are causing a good deal of anguish on the part of some."

His reference was to the *Services for Trial Use*, sometimes called simply "The Green Book." It was a

The General Convention. . . in 1970 committed all Episcopalians to some kind of "Trial" for 1970-73.

preliminary publication of what became the 1979 *Book of Common Prayer*, replacing the 1928 Prayer Book. Its publication fostered the organization of The Prayer Book Society, which still exists.

Inflation and the oil crisis wreaked havoc again in the mid-1970s.

In some regards, the 1970s were the decade when women's roles changed at St. John's. The Vestry had a woman member for the first time. Mrs. W. D. Sutliffe was elected in 1969. The needlepoint project, instigated and designed by Indie Cockerham in 1972, was a major effort

"Penny" with Indie Cockerham

involving many women to create kneelers for the three altars, litany desk, clergy stalls, and sanctuary.

In 1970, the Women of St. John's helped to engineer a family evening, with a spaghetti supper and the documentary film "When Hair Came to Memphis." They helped the office staff to prepare a Parish directory and paid half the cost for the project.

The St. John's Endowment Fund was established in 1973, and contained approximately $83,300. The Vestry, who have responsibility for the Fund, unanimously agreed that the income not be spent for normal operating expenses.

The year 1973 began with $7,564.62 carried forward toward the $200,000 annual budget. There were 1,099

> *"St. John's is a wealthy parish, in terms of committed people, talented and resourceful people, concerned and loyal people; it is also rich in tradition and in courage to face the needs around us."*

members in good standing. The Faith Alive Weekend was inaugurated that May, with the help of nearly 200 parishioners who were involved in planning and preparing for it. In his Annual Report for 1973, Senior Warden Edward H. Newell said that, "St. John's is a wealthy parish, in terms of committed people, talented and resourceful people, concerned and loyal people; it is also rich in tradition and in courage to face the needs around us."

The schedule for services changed again that year. The 9:00 a.m. and 11:00 a.m. services on Sundays were combined into a 10:30 a.m. service. The early and evening celebrations of the Eucharist, at 7:15 a.m. and 5:30 p.m.,

Ordination of The Rev. Mr. Frederick B. Northup

were continued. A third clergyman joined the staff in July, when The Rev. Mr. Frederick B. Northup came as Deacon-in-Training. When Mrs. Reece retired and Mrs. Stafford resigned, the administrative staff and Vestry were evaluated by Mr. Tom Quackenboss, a management consultant, resulting in establishment of an Executive Committee.

The Adult Christian Education schedule continued to offer traditional courses such as *The Old Testament* and *Biblical Man's Experience with God* sprinkled among more of-the-decade titles such as *Religious Faith and Practice of*

"Aunt Trudy" Lott had been at St. John's for 56 years.

Parent and Child in the Modern World, *A Christian Encounter Group*, and *Open Marriage*. Traditional St. John's, like many other mainstream churches, sought to keep pace with change.

People were segmented into the current marketing target groups: Singles, The Elderly, Married Couples, and The Youth.

Reporting at the Annual Parish Meeting, Nathan C. Acree, Senior Warden, described the upheaval of 1974 as "unseating of a president, rising crime rate, real and unreal shortages and crises."

The Rev. Mr. George C. Gibson went to St. Paul's, Memphis, in 1974; The Rev. Mr. Frederick B. Northup went to the American Cathedral in Paris; and in 1975 The Rev. Mr. Noble Ray Walker came to St. John's.

"Aunt Trudy" Lott celebrated her 90th birthday with 125 people attending the party. She had been at St. John's for 56 years.

Both the Rector and The Rev. Mr. George Gibson, Associate Rector, were active in organizing and participating

The Rev. George Calvin Gibson (left) and The Rev. Mr. Frederick B. Northup

in a new neighborhood ecumenical movement called "Cluster of Churches."

In the mid-1970s, the decrease in the number of members in good standing reflected a conscientious effort to correct the records. Many names of people who no

But the Parish, rich in history and possibility, was not growing.

longer lived in the parish were still included on the rolls. Although it appears that the membership dropped considerably during the decade, the actual change was not a dramatic drop as reflected in the revised rolls.

But the Parish, rich in history and possibility, was not growing.

Madge Clark was Hostess for the Parish, and reported that the pot luck suppers during the summer were successful. There was, however, a marked decrease in the number of meals served, since the Men's Club did not meet.

The Men's Club started again in 1977, with a group of about six ladies volunteering to cook and serve the dinner. John Franklin volunteered to grill steaks or chicken, starting a tradition. The Men's Club was reorganized with a large percent of younger—under age 35—men as members. A highlight of the year was a joint dinner meeting with the Women of the Church for a panel presentation on the proposed division of the Diocese.

The First Sunday in Advent, the Sunday nearest to St. Andrew's Day (the patron saint of men and boys), was chosen as the time for the Annual Corporate Communion of the Men and Boys of the Episcopal Church. At St. John's,

the annual observance at the early service is followed by breakfast. Sponsored jointly by the Men's Club and the Laymen of Tennessee, it became traditional for the loose offering to go to the Laymen of the Diocese.

The Men's Club gave a scholarship to a Young People's Service League Camp each year, sending several of the young people to camp.

Dinners and other Parish events were under the capable direction of Louise Hoyt. She says that "It's hard to remember when I stopped being a volunteer and became really staff. When Penny called me in the early 1970s he

"But I love it; been here now for over 20 years."

asked me just to come help out. Even when I began to be paid—after about two years—I still worked more as a volunteer than a part-time employee. But I love it; been here now for over 20 years."

Mrs. Richard J. Reynolds, Jr. (left) and Mrs. Louise Hoyt

At the Annual Parish Meeting on January 16, 1977, plans were begun for a gala celebration of the Parish's 50th anniversary and 100th anniversary as a mission. The dating was made from some old histories of the Parish. The Rev. Mr. Noble R. Walker, Associate Rector, praised the lay leadership and transgenerational events at St. John's. But the membership had dropped to 994,

"I've always tried to look on life, both on the spiritual and physical plane, as an ever growing, ever changing process. . . ."

while the budget grew to $222,382.70. An unprecedented deficit of $18,500 in November precipitated an appeal to the Parish and resulted in such a generous response that the actual deficit for the year was reduced to less than $1,200.

Mr. William T. Edge, Jr. resigned as Scoutmaster of Troop #42, after 25 years, and took on leadership of the Men's Club. Lawrence Rainer came to the staff as a part-time Coordinator of Parish Visiting.

The mid-year meeting of the Parish was inaugurated.

In his report for 1977 to the Annual Parish Meeting, The Rev. Mr. Noble R. Walker, Associate Rector wrote:

Dear People of God at St. John's:

I've always tried to look on life, both on the spiritual and physical plane, as an ever growing, ever changing process. . . .

The E.C.W. sponsored a new project in 1977, and, with good response from the congregation, made $800 on

Mrs. Joseph H. Miller, Jr., Mrs. Harry A. Ramsey, Jr. and "Penny"

a first-ever rummage sale. Eleanor Miller, President, reported that $500 of the earnings went to the "Christmas Store," through which the Churches and Social Services Fund provides Christmas gifts for needy children.

Also in 1977, E.C.W. involved several hundred women in assembling, sorting, and testing over a thousand recipes to create a collection of 410 in *The Recipes According To St. John's*. Seed money of $3,000 advanced by the Vestry to fund the project was repaid in two months of sales, with 800 copies sold. It was the equivalent success to the previous cookbook printed 50 years prior.

...all times for study, meditation, and spiritual growth.

The Centennial Celebration made 1978 a festival year. It began with a Festival Eucharist on Sunday, April 16 and continued for a week-long celebration of 100 years of known history. The week included a musical, luncheon, family dinner, arts and crafts show, and a concert by Dr. & Mrs. Richard Reynolds. Reunion with former parishioners and staff highlighted the celebration. Bayard Morgan, Jennifer Smith, Richard Walker, and Mary McDonnell watered a tree planted in honor of the children. The E.C.W., led by President Fran Catmur, hosted a citywide "Centennial Celebration" on April 18, 1978, with a luncheon, tours of the church, a lecture on the murals, organ demonstrations, and art shows.

The Recipes According to St. John's went to press for the second printing.

Fellowship strengthened through such occasions as Kanuga Conference, Centerpoint, and Quiet Days—all times for study, meditation, and spiritual growth. Ronald

Prothero, new Cub Master, continued the tradition of excellence and St. John's Cub Scout unit, Pack #42, qualified as a National Honor Unit based on quality and leadership, won first-place ribbons at the annual Chickasaw Council Scout Exhibition and annual Camporee, and earned the National Summertime Pack Award. Pack #42 represents the diversity of the city, in membership and in leadership, not only composed of Scouts in the Parish.

With the impetus of the 1978 affirmations, The Rev. Mr. Pennepacker recommended to the next Annual Parish Meeting:

1) Some annual event, not fund-raising, for fellowship.

2) Serious individual ministry of each parishioner.

3) That "[we are] a servant church. We exist for others . . . called to minister to our community, our nation, and the world. We are to build up our own church family in order that we may serve others in Christ's name."

A logical response to the first recommendation was extension of the Centennial Celebration by continuing and expanding the annual Fall Festival. It was a weekend of worship, activities, fun, reunion, and sales. The

"... a servant church. We exist for others ... called to minister to our community, our nation, and the world."

public was invited to share tours of the church; lectures on the murals and architecture; booths with homemade foods, arts, crafts, and handmade children's clothes; horticulture and flower arranging; Christmas decorations; unusual gifts; and cooking demonstrations. Luncheons in the Parish Hall. Hot dogs, popcorn, and soft drinks sold

St. John's Episcopal Church is dedicated to taking the Christian Spirit into the community by helping people. The parish has a responsibility, not only to itself, but to the world around it. Problems of people are also problems of St. John's. Many individuals and groups in the parish are involved in meeting community needs and the problems of those that are in need. Projects are listed below. It is hoped that every member will realize his or her responsiblity to become involved. The rewards are well worth the effort!

OUTREACH PROJECTS

Barth House. *Meals are prepared by Women of the Church for Memphis State University students.*

Clothes Closet. *Clothes are collected for students at Hanley School, the PTA Clothes Closet, Juvenile Court, Shelby County Jail, Transitional House, Youth Services, and other families connected with St. John's.*

Church Women United. *Parish members of CWU collect eye glasses, lenses and frames for the needy. Stamps are collected to be used for purchase of surplus food.*

Hanley School. *Members provide field trips, cultural programs, personal attention, Christmas gifts and clothing to students, many of whom are disadvantaged.*

Muscular Dystrophy Christmas Party. *Sponsored by members of St. John's Episcopal Young Churchmen and Crusaders.*

Scouts. *Cub Scout pack with four dens provided for boys from many parts of the city. Programs include recreation and participation in special environmental "clean-up" projects. The pack has won many scouting awards.*

Shelby County Hospital. *Members visit the hospital once a month to bring cheer to the patients.*

Shelby County Women's Jail Program. *Parish women participate in religious services at the jail with inmates. They teach knitting and crocheting, and collect books and magazines for the women in the jail.*

Sports. *Softball and basketball teams for boys from poverty areas.*

Transitional House for Women. *Members assist in supporting programs of the House that help women recently released from jail.*

Youth Services. *Women of the parish provide lunches at the center. Lunches help bring together military personnel and young boys.*

The parish also supports the following programs with financial assistance from the St. John's Memorial Trust Fund.

PROJECTS FUNDED IN 1974

Hanley School Summer Reading Program for 1st and 2nd graders. ($400)
Baseball Uniforms for Tillman-Binghamton Service Center team. ($60)
Youth Service Summer Recreation Program for girls form the Orange Mound Area ($350)
Tillman-Binghamton Clinic equipment ($500)
Big Brothers of Memphis ($250)
Crisis and Suicide Prevention Center ($600)
Cluster of Churches Day Care Center ($250)
Churches and Social Services providing emergency aid to persons who are referred by a clergyman ($350)

PROJECTS FUNDED IN 1975

Youth Services Summer Recreation Program. Second year ($500)
Big Brothers of Memphis. Second year ($1000)
Furnishings for Women's Transition Center house ($1000)
Crisis and Suicide Prevention Center. Second year ($700)
Vietnamese family sponsored by Cluster of Churches ($250)
Southwestern WLYX Radio Readers serving the blind and print handicapped people in Memphis ($400)

PROJECTS FUNDED IN 1976

Memphis Ecumenical Childrens' Association group homes for neglected children of Shelby County ($1000)
St. Francis Home for Boys ($200)

in the courtyard by the Men's Club. Music. Entertainment for children.

Mrs. E. Alan Catmur (Fran) was chairman. Altar Guild members Mrs. Paul Gillespie (Dottie) and Mrs. Hal Bailey (Diana) were co-chairmen for church tours. Mrs. Wallace Pennepacker (Frances) was overall chairman for booths, assisted by Mrs. Richard Walker, Mrs. Richard Reynolds, Mrs. Edward Newell, Mrs. Harry Ramsay, and Mrs. Richard Patterson. Mrs. Herbert Humphreys decorated the library for the booths. Mrs. Guy Robbins, cooking chairman, demonstrated Chinese cooking, Mrs. Eugart Yerian demonstrated French cooking, and Mrs. Harry Bass demonstrated Greek cooking. Mrs. Goodloe Early, Mrs. Louise Hoyt, Mrs. Albert Mallory, III, and Mrs. Thomas Karydis accomplished luncheon for the dozens who purchased tickets at $3.75. Mrs. Joseph Miller, Mrs. James McGehee, Mrs. Robert G. Snowden, Mrs. R. G. Moxley, Mrs. William Leatherman, and Mrs. Roy Creson (overall chairman) managed the horticulture and flower arranging events. John Pierce gave a demonstration on pruning. Martha Miller headed up the Youth Groups, who painted clown faces on children. All combined to be the kick-off of a fund raiser that brings in about $15,000 each year.

As the 1970s were ending, the staff changed again. Gloria Jackson, assistant to D.C.E. The Rev. Mr. Noble Walker, married and moved to Louisiana. She was replaced by Mrs. Joseph W. Barnwell, Jr. (Gayle).

Boy Scout Troop #42

18

During Lent in 1981, The Right Reverend John M. Allin, Presiding Bishop, wrote for the St. John's bulletin:

Beloved in Christ,

It is not comfortable to be a Christian in every part of this world. We are reminded of that as we approach another Good Friday, and our thoughts are drawn to the lands that Jesus knew so well. Some of these lands are in turmoil today . . . Tensions continue between Arabs and Israelis. Lebanon bows to civil strife. Ethiopia wars against Somalia. Iraq clashes with Iran. . . .

Fifteen years later the list of battlefronts expands to the Balkans, unfortunately not decreased by peaceful settlement in any of the above list, but with the long tragedy of the former Yugoslavia added. Rwanda.

As with missions, now with war. No longer foreign only, but a War on Poverty, War on Drugs, gang wars, drive-by shootings, weapons searches in elementary schools. Carjackings. Abductions that made The Good Samaritan passe. Panhandlers at the church steps, heaping guilt on parishioners as they leave worship. An estimated homeless population of more than 10,000 in Memphis by the early 1990s—the so-called "invisible" population not reflected in the 1990 U.S. Census figures.

In 1984, *Life* magazine said that one out of three people in the world was Christian. Churches, however—especially mainstream Protestant churches—sought new ways to meet the needs of congregations, to improve programs, to increase attendance, to fund the ever-increasing budget.

Marshall S. Scott became Associate Rector in 1981, working with youth and acting as mentor to part-time seminarian Vincent Ciamaritaro.

Betty Robinson created the little folder on symbols, to be placed in card racks for newcomers and parishioners to understand the iconography in the church.

Division of the Diocese of Tennessee was approved at the 1982 General Convention in New Orleans, and took

"It is not comfortable to be a Christian in every part of this world."

place January 1, 1983. The actual division had been voted at a prior Convention in Nashville—not without some rancor. Bishop Gates presided over the first Convention of the Diocese of West Tennessee, at which The Rev. Mr. Alex D. Dickson was elected the first Bishop.

The Endowment Trust was established in 1984 with $425,000 from the Estate of Mary Lou Brown.

Following the retirement of The Rev. Mr.

Vestry Retreat

Pennepacker in 1983, the search for his replacement took months longer than anticipated. At that point, St. John's Episcopal Church had been in a position of stable leadership for decades, with only two rectors during the 55 years since recognition as a Parish in 1928. Although The Rev. Mr. Pennepacker gave six months' notice, it was more than a year before The Rev. Mr. Stewart Wood became Rector in October 1984.

The 1984 income from the Brown Fund was $30,000, and it was decided to use half of the earnings, with 25% for capital improvements, 25% for outreach. A gift of $22,500 to the Irene Rogers Beasley Fund was also announced at the Annual Meeting. E.C.W. cleared $6,050 in 1984 and $6,500 in 1985 on Fall Festival.

In 1985 the Youth Commission set a goal to try to reactivate Crusaders (junior high age) and to field at least one basketball team. The Commission worked to design a youth program that would attract new interest, and looked for new leadership to replace Vincent Ciamaritaro, who went to study at Sewanee. The Parish presented him with a check in appreciation of his work as Youth Director.

A new pictorial directory in 1985 replaced a prior one made in 1978.

Mid-decade was a time of restructuring, with St. John's changing in 1985 to the Commission System, patterned somewhat after a system traditionally used in the Methodist Church. Many other changes were administrative, with new computers, new regulations for cash management, a safe to secure offerings, and insurance for staff. Semantics changed; "Chairman" became "Convener." The Rev. Mr. Wood worked for summer term toward a degree

Betty Robinson's Brochure

from Virginia Seminary. In June 1985 the Vestry recommended Battle Beasley to Bishop Alex Dickson as a candidate for Holy Orders.

Annie's Nannies approached St. John's about the prospect of starting a daycare center, but the Vestry did not feel that having the commercial venture use the space was appropriate. When the Junior League requested permission in 1987 to organize a Mother's Day Out program at St. John's, it seemed a better fit. Once the program was well established, the League, fulfilling their mission statement, turned to other projects, and St. John's continues sponsorship for the program. It has expanded each year, serving those who need safe care in a non-profit financial structure as well as caring for children of the Parish.

A gift from Elizabeth and Bayard Boyle to have hollies planted across the back of the parking lot started 1986 well. It was, however, a year of problems and dissent.

The budget needed to be reduced by $100,000. A new

A Vestry Weekend planning session

security system was necessary, after a theft of $10,000. (The thieves were apprehended when police noticed that the car was riding extremely low, and discovered the brasses from the church.) The Church School Education program and proposed new by-laws for the national church generated controversy.

The ordination of women, the acceptance of the new Prayer Book, the Church's position on abortion, and new

But a new provision decreed that an Episcopal Church was always an Episcopal Church.

language to accommodate what would later be termed "politically correct" terminology presented schismatic ideology. Some Episcopal congregations wanted to leave the Episcopal Church, taking with them the property of the Parish. But a new provision decreed that an Episcopal Church was always an Episcopal Church.

Another divisive debate was the budget. The Vestry passed a budget for 1987 with more than $6,000 deficit after a motion for a balanced budget failed.

Problems were the impetus for reassessment. The Vestry Planning weekend in 1986 concluded:

1) Strengths were proximity of a concentrated population, beautiful buildings, warm people, good leadership, four Sunday services.

2) Concerns were a building that was too large; trends in giving; need for improved communications; a need to build young leadership.

A long-range planning retreat at St. Columba the following February addressed the problems, defining goals:

I. Capital funds, with a long-range plan for capital improvements; a committee was formed to propose a plan.

II. Staff realignment, with increased clergy (a second priest) and decreased staff, supplemented by volunteers.

III. Greater Parish involvement, led by a highly visible Rector; better communication.

IV. Strengthened basic loyalties, with realistic expectation and accountability of volunteers; assessment of a Commission system.

It became a time of consultants for staffing, funding, and working together.

The Rev. Mr. Noble Walker returned temporarily as priest for the 5:30 p.m. Sunday service. In mid-year Tom Hotchkiss arrived to work with youth and young adults. Originally from Washington, D.C., he graduated from Vanderbilt and worked with Young Life in Nashville and Memphis before coming to St. John's. The Rev. Mrs. Iris R. Slocombe, a former neurological surgical nurse, was called to St. John's as the Rector's Associate.

Attempts to re-create community led to family dinners, young adult supper clubs, notes to newcomers and parishioners with special needs. Committees were organized to greet newcomers after the 11 o'clock Sunday service, and to make hospital calls. Friends of Music was organized in 1987. The church sponsored a Polish refugee family. There were four T-ball teams. Fall Festival earned $6,200.

Some of the activities that were organized did not materialize: not enough people signed up for a ski trip to Gatlinburg.

Scores of people signed up to form the 14 committees preparing for the Fifth annual West Tennessee Diocesan Convention, hosted by St. John's January 14-16, 1988. Bishop Sanders preached at the opening Eucharist. His portrait, painted by Billy Price Carroll, was unveiled at the reception following. Billy told that her sister, Nadia (a renowned photographer), said, "Billy, you'll never get him." But Billy has a reputation for catching a likeness of her subjects, and when she finished the portrait, Nadia said, "Billy, you got him!"

From the opening Eucharist, reception, luncheon, dinner dance, and sessions to the closing Eucharist, St. John's committees worked. Jack Bugbee, June Wilcox, Clark Taylor, Malissa Jones, Lou Hoyt, Hilda Lewis, Mimi

Attempts to re-create community led to family dinners, young adult supper clubs, notes to newcomers and parishioners with special needs.

Mallory, Art Mayhall, Tom Hotchkiss, Bill Gillaspie, Harry Wilcox, Joe Snider, John Barbee, Fitzhugh Taylor, Bill Belcher, Oliver Jeanes, and John Ayer led groups of Parishioners eager to provide hospitality to the Convention.

Issues at the Convention were human sexuality, inclusive language (for acknowledging a divergent community), and reports from commissions on alcoholism and abortion. All were issues that became more rather than less difficult in coming years.

The Rev. Mr. Stewart Wood announced in February 1988 that he was a candidate for Bishop of Michigan. He was elected and moved from Memphis in August. The Rev. Mr. Noble Walker again officiated at the Sunday evening service and made hospital calls, assisted by Frank Donelson doing East Memphis visits mid-week.

The Elizabeth Mitchell Fund was established to underwrite the needs of the choir, acolytes, and Vestry. A gift of $6,150 was designated for refurbishing the Church.

In 1988, Jesse Jackson was the first serious black contender for President of the United States.

The budget for 1989 was "pared down" from $610,825 to $578,525, although the original amount was deemed necessary to fund the needs for the year. In November 1989, Ann Reynolds was honored for 50 years in the choir. Also that year, the Women of St. John's gave $3,000 toward the Memphis Boy Choir's concert tour.

Membership declined over the period 1980-89, but the number of dollars pledged increased. The budget was still a problem, running to nearly $40,000 deficit at one time. Each time there was a financial crunch, an appeal to the membership narrowed the gap between income and expenses; it didn't change the trend.

For the Protestant Episcopal Church as a whole, baptized membership grew 36.7% between 1926 (about the time The Rev. Mr. Loaring-Clark began at St. John's) and 1950 (just over a year before his death). In 1983, membership was only 19% more than in 1950, although it had been greater before beginning to decline in the 1960s. Membership for all Protestant denominations in the U.S. was 48,853,367 in 1953, grew 50% by 1983, and is estimated to be almost doubled in 1996, with evangelical denominations as the fastest growing. Huston Smith's 1958 book, *The Religions of Man*, showed more diversity of belief among Christian denominations, with the belief in

Membership for all Protestant denominations in the U.S. was 48,853,367 in 1953, grew 50% by 1983

the divinity of Christ as the only unifying element in structure, than between Christianity and some other religions.

Some of the changes in membership of all churches in the U.S. (not just Protestant) are directly related to changes in demographics over the past 40 years. Surveys show that the Boomer generation tends to be less involved with mainstream religion than their parents; the large influx of immigrants from non-Protestant cultures affects the growth rate; and migrant lifestyles magnify detachment.

For St. John's, the decade of the 1990s began with renewal.

From the constant change of the 1980s, the search committee for a new rector sought constancy, reconciliation, and charismatic, congenial leadership. Chaired by Jim Russell, the committee carefully interviewed, visited, and assessed candidates, finally focusing on a "hometown boy" who seemed extremely well-qualified and a good fit with the needs of the Parish. The Rev. Dr. James M. Coleman was called in November 1988. With his wife (Mary Carter Hughes of Gallatin) and three grown sons (James, Carter, and Jonathan) he relocated back to his hometown. He seemed just the right leader for St. John's and his first Sunday would be March 5, 1989. He would be elected Bishop of the Diocese of West Tennessee only four years later—the first native-born Tennessean to serve as bishop of any diocese since the Diocese of Tennessee was founded in 1834.

James Malone Coleman was born in Memphis and graduated from Christian Brothers High School. After a stint in the Army, he earned a B.S. in journalism from the

The "old" Memphis Boys' Choir, 1948

. . . focusing on a "hometown boy. . ."

University of Tennessee. Changing course, he earned a Master of Divinity degree from University of the South, and took his doctorate in Pastoral Theology from the Baptist Seminary at Wake-Forest. He served parishes in Gallatin and Lebanon, Tennessee; was chaplain at Georgia Tech and Agnes Scott; and was Rector at churches in Knoxville and Johnson City, Tennessee; Martinsville, Virginia; and Baton Rouge, Louisiana before returning to

Memphis. He has been on boards of schools, the YMCA, Urban Ministries, and as a Trustee of Sewanee. In the Diocese of Tennessee he served on the Board of Examining Chaplains, the Diocesan Liturgical Committee, the Committee on Ministry, and other committments.

It was no longer standard for the Assistant Rector to be considered for Rector in an Episcopal church, and The Rev. Mrs. Iris Slocum stayed as Priest-in-Charge through the months the church had no Rector. She was offered the opportunity to remain at St. John's as Director of Religious Education, but wrote to The Rev. Dr. Jim Coleman that she "felt called to sacramental ministry," and resigned in May 1989 after being called to Grace Church in Mount Clemens, Michigan.

Many changes occurred in 1989-90. The 40-year-old buildings needed renovation and an anonymous gift of $20,000 through the Capital Gifts fund made possible the completion of the tower project. The Vestry elected to have a professional fundraiser to organize an official Capital Funds Campaign. The new Rector made a strong statement that he did not favor deficit financing. Growth resumed.

July 1989 was a turning point. Although income during summer months was traditionally low, receipts in July exceeded expenses.

Although the Vestry felt a "dire need" for an Assistant Rector, The Rev. Dr. Jim Coleman said he would like

With overwhelming response, the budget was restored.

the position funded first. It happened quickly. Pledges for 1990 were up $40,000 over 1989.

The capital improvements needs grew to be almost $2,000,000. The Vestry approved borrowing up to $600,000 to complete the capital improvements campaign until sufficient capital pledges were received.

The income budget made it necessary to cut $5,000 from the Diocesan pledge, and the Parish and staff resisted. The Rev. Dr. Jim Coleman said that he had never had to make such a budget cut, appealing to the Parish to prevent such a drastic measure. With overwhelming response, the budget was restored.

The Rev. Mr. Joseph N. Davis came as Assistant Rector. John Ayer was able to hire soloists as section leaders for the choir. Contributions to the Church Health Center and other outreach programs increased.

Mid-1989 The Rev. Dr. Jim Coleman suggested that the Men's Club take on the responsibility for taping the 11:00 a.m. service each Sunday and make it available for shut-ins to borrow.

Bill Murray, Jennifer Smith, and Tom and Marcia Hotchkiss went to St. John's companion diocese in Barbados on an exchange program in the summer of 1990. About 40 young people worked on a house in North Memphis for Neighborhood Housing Opportunities. T-Ball, softball, volleyball, and basketball teams were organized. Youth groups sold Christmas trees and wreaths as a fund-raising project. Youth Service leased space on the third floor.

The Diocese formed "Cluster Groups" of churches to promote mutual learning among similar churches. St. John's was assigned to Cluster #2, with St. Mary's Cathedral, Holy Trinity, Holy Apostles, and St. Elizabeth's.

African Team Ministries asked permission, granted, to send handicrafts for sale as a funding project for mission work in Africa.

The 1990 goals encouraging fiscal responsibility and more lay ministry were met.

By 1991 there were 72 children signed up for T-ball—50% of whom were non-members.

Tom Hotchkiss left to enter Virginia Theological Seminary, speeded with The Rev. Dr. Jim Coleman's encouragement. In his first year at St. John's, The Rev. Dr. Jim Coleman gave his share of money from the Crawford account—earmarked for continuing education for the staff—to enable Tom to attend the summer session at Fuller Seminary in Colorado Springs, completing his M.A. in Religion with emphasis on Youth Ministry.

The Youth and Young Adult Committee, chaired by Lucy Miller, drew up a job description for a new Youth Director. Van Gurney fit the criteria, and was hired in September 1991.

The Rev. Dr. Jim Coleman was elected President of the Diocese of West Tennessee Clerics in the fall of 1991, expanding his leadership.

New programs, improved finances, attendance, and growth marked 1992. The Stephen Ministry program began, Vacation Bible School resumed after a 6-year absence, a widening bridge of income over expenses made it possible to reduce the debt for capital improvements, attendance in Sunday School required more staffing, and the

New programs, improved finances, attendance, and growth marked 1992.

1993 pledge goal of $550,000 was reached. At the Diocesan Convention, Jim Russell was elected (for the third time) as lay deputy to the General Convention held in Indianapolis in 1994.

Issues for the Church generally still generated heated controversy—such as the recurrent divisive debates over sex, gender, and abortion issues. For St. John's, though, the Parish had achieved restoration for the buildings and the organ, renewed commitment from the membership.

Change came again in June 1993 when The Rev. Dr. Jim Coleman was elected Bishop of the Diocese of West Tennessee.

Strength for the New Century

19

At the middle of the last decade in this century, St. John's is regrouping, preparing for the new century. With new staff for the beginning of 1996 and the Fall Festival raising nearly $15,000, the Parish moves forward in strength. But, as the Rector reported at the January Annual Meeting, "The year 1995 has not been an easy one . . . but . . . it offers . . . a good foundation upon which to build." With a staff who, except for John Ayer, have not been at St. John's very long, tradition and continuity depended upon people like John Allen, Father Don Mowery, and Frank Donelson, who bridged the void in clerical leadership during the period when there was no rector.

Following the leap in membership of the Protestant Episcopal Church in America between 1926 and 1950—

"The year 1995 has not been an easy one . . . but . . . it offers . . . a good foundation upon which to build."

roughly parallelling the years when The Rev. Mr. Alfred Loaring-Clark was Rector—and deceleration and decline during the next three decades, by the 1990s, membership did not equate to attendance.

By mid-decade of the 1990s, David Yount, writing for Scripps Howard News Service announced that church-going had "dropped to a new low . . . with only 37% of Americans (attending weekly)." He noted, however, that there was no correlation with church attendance and faith, as reported in religious surveys. Although fewer people attend church on Sunday, polls indicate that "94% of Americans believe in God and . . . 75% pray . . . daily."

At St. John's, the changes formed new alliances. In 1991, June Wilcox retired from supervising Sunday flower deliveries. This is now under direction of ECW, with a different chapter responsible each Sunday, according to a calendar published in the ECW yearbook.

In 1992, the Men's Club joined with Women of the Church to put an advertisement in *The Commercial Appeal* Religious News each week, giving times and place for St. John's services.

That year the Archbishop of Kenya and his wife visited St. John's for four days.

In 1994, the Vestry search committee selected The Rev. Mr. Noland Pipes as next rector for St. John's. He had earned a B.A. at Virginia Military Institute and B.D. at the University of the South. He was assistant to the headmaster, The Rev. Mr. Alex Dockery Dickson, Jr., at All Saints Episcopal School in Vicksburg, Mississippi, before coming to Memphis in 1991 as rector at the Church of the Annunciation in Cordova.

John Allen became Administrator in January 1994. Ted Schurch came in March 1995 as Director of Christian

Education; The Rev. Mr. Myron Manasterski arrived as Assistant Rector. The Rev. Mr. John Sterling and Father Don Mowery filled in until the new Rector, The Rev. Mr. Noland Pipes, arrived in July 1994. St. John's hosted the Diocesan Convention again in 1994.

Ted Schurch began his report for 1995 with thanks that he had been called to serve as Director of Christian Education and Coordinator of Youth Ministry. He called St. John's "an exciting and growing parish that is beginning to realize its great potential."

The year began with 1,047 members, and a total budget over $600,000. With a core group of faithful and committed communicants, St. John's Parish marches into the new century with momentum.

The Fall Festival continues to be rewarding financially and a time for reunion with former parishioners.

...new leadership from The Rev. Mr. Noland Pipes, Rector, and continuity of faith move the Parish toward new challenges in the 21st Century.

Net profit from the festival has ranged from $19,000 to $7,700, when reduced space due to renovations diminished possibility for exhibits. Proceeds from Fall Festival have been used to help furnish the nursery and Mother's Day Out; to furnish the new Bride's Room; and to fund many outreach projects.

Men of St. John's have traditionally attended and supported the annual conference each year of the Episcopal Churchmen of Tennessee, held at DuBose Conference Center at Monteagle. During August 1996 the Episcopal Churchmen of Tennessee will celebrate their Golden

Men's Conference attending All Saints Church in Sewanee, Tennessee

Anniversary, called "The Year of the Jubilee: Celebration and Forgiveness."

New staff, new leadership from The Rev. Mr. Noland Pipes, Rector, and continuity of faith move the Parish toward new challenges in the 21st Century. Many of the new opportunities will be funded by income from the careful stewardship of trust funds.

The Alfred Loaring-Clark Memorial Fund

The Alfred Loaring-Clark Memorial Fund was established in November 1969 with an initial donation of $5,000 from Mr. & Mrs. Sam Carey. A committee is elected at annual Parish meetings, and charged with recommending to the Vestry how the fund income is allocated. For the first two decades, the principal could not be used, but, beginning in January 1990, up to 10 percent of principal could be used per year.

The trust is established so that additional gifts are added to the principal. Income from the fund is specified for mission projects, either foreign or domestic; for training for work in missions; and for work among youth, the elderly, minority, or other needy groups.

The Irene Rogers Beasley Mission Fund

At the same time, the Careys established the Irene Rogers Beasley Mission Fund, also with an initial donation of $5,000. Rules for use of the fund are the same as for the Loaring-Clark Trust.

The Cemetery Fund

From 1979 to 1982, gifts from James D. Robinson provided funds to purchase and maintain the cemetery at the northeast corner of Central Avenue and Lafayette Drive. A Trust established in 1982 governs the principal, which totaled $450,000 in donations, and manages the cemetery for the benefit of St. John's.

The Mitchell Vestment Account

The family of Elizabeth Mitchell started the Mitchell Vestment Account with $10,000 to be invested and $5,000 to be used immediately to furnish altar hangings and other vestments used for the worship service. With the addition of a previous altar vestment account added to the principal, upon instructions from the rector, the principal invested totaled $14,882.

Dr. P. Thurman Crawford Memorial Fund

Mrs. Thurman Crawford established the memorial fund to Dr. Crawford with an original contribution of $10,000. This fund is allocated for educational expenses of the Clergy and staff.

History Fund

Mrs. James Robinson (Martha) established the History Fund to underwrite the preparation and publication of the Church History begun by Mrs. Wallace Pennepacker (Frances). Originally funded at $15,000, the disbursements from both principal and interest were to be used at the discretion of Mrs. Pennepacker, with approval of the Rector.

Mary Louise Prewitt Memorial Fund

Established November 20, 1985 by a gift from the family of Mary Louise Prewitt, the initial principal of this fund was $20,000. Specifically, the purpose of the fund was "to benefit worthy individuals and/or organizations in the hope that some of the effects of suffering, poverty and economic misfortune can be alleviated." Four additional gifts in 1985-88 brought the principal to $95,000. The annual income from the fund is administered by the treasurer, with advice from the Investment Committee. The guidelines from the family stipulate that principal will not be used.

Lecture Series Fund

A gift from Elinor Turner established the Lecture Series Fund in 1986. Additional amounts from memorial donations brought the principal to $20,000. Income from the fund is used to provide speakers for special lecture series, such as the LeFebvre Lecture Series in 1987.

In 1938, The Rev. Mr. Alfred Loaring-Clark wrote:
Like a stream coursing down the centuries, gathering new clearness and strength from its tributaries, the church must move forward. We would pray that as a congregation and as individuals, our vision of God increases with the years.

Reminiscences

Appendix 1

*I*n the early 1980s, Frances Pennepacker organized more than 100 people into teams to interview long-time parishioners about their reminiscences of St. John's. The transcripts of the interviews total hundreds of pages, characterized by fascinating stories, very personal expressions of warmth, love, faith, and a familial attitude toward the church.

The following excerpts from transcripts and letters give glimpses of the legacy of faith exemplified throughout nearly a century and a half.

Most of those interviewed referred to the two rectors they knew longest by their nicknames, as if they were family members. These quotes and paraphrases reflect those original statements.

Louise Moore

I was confirmed at St. John's in 1925, after attending first Buntyn Presbyterian then Prescott Memorial Baptist with my parents. Everyone loved St. John's because it was a closely knit congregation. The church had a little pot-bellied stove that the men and boys stoked. They also pumped the organ while the organist played.

Marian Scrivener Bodenheimer

Sometimes when I put on my light-as-air summer garments and go in air-conditioned car to air-conditioned church, I distinctly remember summers in the 1920s. Even though I was in scanty child's attire, I remember the discomfort of perspiration rolling down and soaking my Sunday socks. Remember, people wore *clothes* in those days, especially the men. The more affluent had "Palm Beach" suits, but those starched high collars, stiff wide cuffs, and neckties must have been a mild form of Christian martyrdom. The women's martyrdom was not visible, but equally or more torturous.

David Fox

The fire in the old church buildings took place two days before Christmas, 1937. It started in the Vesting Room, destroying all the church records kept there. The fire spread into the Kindergarten room. The only part of the church that was damaged was the wall behind the altar. Pine boughs were used to cover the charred wall, and services were held on Christmas Day in spite of the fire.

William Carmick McCormick, Jr.

When I became associated with St. John's in the mid-1930s, the Rector, Alfred Loaring-Clark, was very dynamic and drew a large, devoted following. We had a regular carpool from Chickasaw Gardens carted there for Sunday School: James Taylor, Robert Wolff, David Taylor, my brother James, and I. Actually, I recall the Sunday School's proximity to the pinball machine, soda fountain, and comic books in the drug store across the street.

In later years it meant the place where the Christmas Eve children's service makes up for the wrong (commercial) emphasis at the end of Advent. And as the dross has been sloughed and truth revealed, St. John's evening mass is quite a welcoming feast, a quiet peace.

Meade Nichol

When we moved to Memphis in 1929, we liked St. John's best of all the Episcopal churches, and Bill had known Tib at Sewanee.

Tib had us all out every day calling on new people.

One of my earliest recollections was helping Irene Beasley with the Lenten Choir. I could not sing, but I was a pretty good disciplinarian and I could teach the children. I could wash and I could iron. A lady across the street washed the vestments and Dale Kerr and I helped iron them.

Harry and Elizabeth Ramsay

(Harry Ramsay's early memories are included in Chapter 6, *Mission*.)

Shortly after Harry and I married in 1934, his mother said that she knew I was going to love St. John's. It was quite a change, since I grew up attending whatever church was near where we lived. After I married and moved to Memphis, I jumped right in to work at St. John's. Bishop Gailor confirmed me and I started teaching a Sunday School class. I served many years on the Altar Guild and in the chapters of the Women of the Church, as well as in Diocesan work. I was organist and choirmaster for a while and sang in the choir after Richard White came.

I especially remember Meade Nichol. One time Meade decided that we should have mashed potatoes for a particular Men's Club dinner. At that time, the kitchen facilities were terrible. We had to cook many things at home, then take them to the church. Meade cooked 30 pounds of potatoes for the dinner, and we had to whip them with a fork!

Katherine Boehme Troth

Dick Boehme and I married in August 1939, and were confirmed at St. John's in December of that year because we both liked The Rev. Mr. Loaring-Clark and all the many young couples we met at the church. I think about how the choir walked down the aisle every Christmas Eve holding lighted candles, and wearing cotton cottas. The whole church was just a wooden structure, packed to the rafters. But there was never a fire caused that way.

I sang in the choir and taught Sunday School (4th grade) for 20 years. The church activities and the ever presence of a priest helped me to endure the grief after my husband's death. I married again and my daughter Katherine Suzanne Troth was christened at the old St. John's, with Elizabeth and Ronald Hopton and Virginia and Oscar Hurt as godparents.

Evelyn Burch

(Mrs. Evelyn Peters Burch, widow of Judge Charles Newell Burch, and formerly Evelyn McNeal Peters, daughter of Attorney General George Boddie Peters and Katie Greenlaw Peters, was born in 1873 and died in 1954. She had one daughter, Mrs. Robert Harvey Nesbit.)

President of the Woman's Auxiliary of St. John's, Diocesan President of the Tennessee Episcopal Woman's Auxiliary, organizer of a local branch of the Young

Women's Christian Association (1918) and its first president, a member of the Canteen Service of the Red Cross, and always with time for young people. She met trains, fed boys and arranged transportation during the first World War, World War II, and the Korean War. Mrs. Burch made several trips through the South, forming units of the American Red Cross. From her debut until her death Mrs. Burch was an indefatigable leader in Memphis' social and religious life.

Mrs. Kenneth Jackson (Elizabeth)

My sister Lucy Willins and I started in the Sunday School when I was about four years old (1911). There were only four or five children there. I remember The Rev. Peter Wager, a kindly gentleman with a grey beard, who at Easter gave me a little cardboard cross with the Beatitudes written on the back, which I have always cherished.

We moved away for awhile, but returned. Lucy, our brother Walker, and I would walk about three-quarters of a mile to catch the street car to go to Sunday School. The Rev. Paul Williams, then the Priest-in-Charge, was a rotund little man with rosy cheeks, glasses, and very blonde hair.

We had picnics at Riverside and Overton parks, Easter egg hunts and taffy pullings at the Farnsworths, Junior Daughters of the King and social gatherings at the Lowrances (who had a player piano that delighted all of the young people).

The next Priest-in-Charge was The Reverend M. L. Tate, who divided his time between St. John's and Holy Trinity. On alternate Sundays we had lay readers, usually Mr. Farnsworth or Mr. Robinson. One Easter there was a four foot cross of flowers made entirely by the children.

Nat and Lydia McConnell

(Nat had been the widower of Eunice McConnell; Lydia had been the widow of Buck Burnette—all faithful members of St. John's.)

Nat: I came to Memphis and St. John's in 1946, prompted to go to St. John's because I had been to the church in Jackson, Tennessee, where the rector was Tib Loaring-Clark's father.

I believe that the quietness and simplicity of ideas created by the Brotherhood of St. Andrew were crucial to the policy St. John's adopted during the troubled times when our city prayed over civil rights. Herbert Jordan was the leader of our group of about 10.

The growth, the friendliness, and the joy of St. John's. . . are led by Wallace Pennepacker, one of the most deeply spiritual men I have ever known.

Lydia: Buck Burnette, our son Bill, and I came to Memphis right after the war and felt so much at home at St. John's.

When Fergus O'Connor came as organist and choir master, he formed a Boys' Choir. Bill, seven at the time, became a member, and Fergus asked me to be the Choir Mother.

After Buck's death, Penny asked me to take over the job as hostess to the church, supervising wedding receptions, luncheons, Men's Club dinners, breakfast during Lent, and any other occasion when meals were served.

Nancy and Ralph Lewis

Nancy: Mother, Daddy, Frances, Emily, Mary, and I moved from Little Rock about 50 years ago, and became involved in the church immediately. Daddy insisted that everyone had to go to church, but we were always late marching in to sit in the front pew.

Daddy was always on the Vestry, and forever worrying whether the church had enough money. Mother belonged to the Woman's Auxiliary (president at one time) and taught Sunday School in the old church.

Ralph: When Mrs. T. K. Robinson collared me, an unchurched person, and asked me to come to Sunday School, I was about in the 10th grade. I became an acolyte, taught Sunday School, and have been going ever since.

The Rev. Mr. Marshall S. Scott

My first visit to St. John's was on Pentecost Sunday in 1981. I had recently been informed by Bishop Sanders that I would be placed there, and, when Valere and I came to house hunt, Wallace invited me to join him for Pentecost services. I remember that we wore matching red stoles that had been made especially for the service by the children in the Sunday School.

I served as Wallace's Associate for two years and four months, until his retirement.

The most notable event was, I think, the gift from the estate of Helen Brown, which was the basis of the Brown Trust. A gentleman called in March, identifying himself as president of the Bank of Henderson, Tennessee, and executor of the estates of Mr. and Mrs. Brown. He informed me of a bequest to St. John's of $425,000 and said he would like to present it at the 11:00 service the following Sunday, which would be April 1. It was not until after he hung up that I realized that it was also April Fools' Day. We waited to see if this magnificent gift would truly appear, and were truly thrilled when it did. The funds were invested by the Vestry, with the income to be divided between outreach and building and grounds maintenance expenses.

Mrs. Giles Coors (Gertrude)

When Dr. Coors and I built the first house on the lake in Chickasaw Gardens (1929), I transferred my church membership from Grace-St. Luke's to tiny St. John's.

My son George remembers riding his pony over and tying him to a wire fence on the north side of the church, while he attended confirmation classes.

Dr. Marcus Stewart

When we came back from Houston after World War II, we visited many different churches. After visiting with Tib Loaring-Clark at the little old frame church at Semmes and Spottswood, we definitely decided that was where we wanted to be. Tib and I both liked to hunt and that gave us a close personal relationship. Also, he always impressed me with the way he would always pick up our oldest child, who was just walking, and kiss her on the cheek.

Mariette Stewart

I remember that in the early 1950s when Chapters were re-organized, I was first Chapter Chairman of a new Chapter called St. Monica's. We were eager to do our part, and would understand and sign up for the nursery and the kitchen duties, or what have you, but when it came time for devotionals, no one felt qualified to give the devotional. For two years, Irene McDonald came to each of our meetings and gave a very inspiring devotional.

Then we had a precious prayer group that included Mary Lee Fulmer, Elinor Turner, Erna Bladow, Virginia Parker, Melda MacDonald, Elizabeth Boyle, Beth Jordan,

Jessie Rogers, Anne Reynolds, and me. Everybody derived a great deal of spiritual good from it.

Jean Bond Clark

I remember that in kindergarten we received pastel ribbons if we could repeat the Bible stories we were told. And there was always a cupcake and thank offering on birthdays.

There was a big Easter Egg Hunt in the two Scrivener yards on Easter Monday. During Lent, sandwiches and cocoa were served before the Sunday evening service.

One of our main youth projects was making money for scholarships to Camp Gailor-Maxon. One year we had a minstrel show. Another year we performed H.M.S. Pinafore, with considerable musical instruction from some members of the adult choir.

The boys in senior high used to really put the teachers on the spot with questions like, "What is heaven like?" But several boys went to seminary because of the tremendous influence Mr. Loaring-Clark had on the teenagers in our group. He was so much admired, loved, and important in all our lives—a friend and leader for all. I do not know of anyone whose life was not made better by his presence and leadership. Every Sunday he came around to each Church School department to greet and say a few words to everyone. He was the heart of St. John's.

Lucille Watkins

Lucille Watkins was a member of St. John's in Aberdeen, Mississippi before joining St. John's in 1946. She helped to vest the Junior Choir, of which her daughter, Whitfield, was a member. She also held every chapter office except devotional chairman.

She served on the kitchen crew under Mrs. Walter Lott. Once she sprained her ankle while carrying food from the little old kitchen across into the dining room.

Virginia Vookles

I remember that John Carey received a gift umbrella for some special occasion, and showed up for Sunday School for weeks—maybe months—with that umbrella, rain or shine.

At the old church, for the children's Thanksgiving service, Mr. Loaring-Clark went through the alphabet and the children called out things to be thankful for, things that began with that letter.

When we moved to the new church, Elizabeth Boyle and I were in charge of the three-year-old nursery, assisted by Mary Napier, Dollie Spalding, Wilda Humphreys, Carrie Wood, Dot Davis, and others. We visited churches all over the city to see what equipment and what materials were being used, and then proceeded to get for our own use what we thought was best. We studied the psychology of working with children, as well as lesson material, and we loved our work.

Ruth Loaring-Clark Mainard

When I went to Memphis to teach at St. Mary's school, my brother was rector of St. John's. I think the date was 1935.

I loved singing in the choir and carolling at Christmas. We had a quartet—Ursi McGinley (our organist then) sang contralto; Raynor Allen, bass; Tib, tenor; and I sang soprano. We went to several houses on Christmas Eve before the service—a rewarding and heart-warming experience.

I remember that at the Thanksgiving service for children, Tib always ended with a "pep talk" on the theme "because we have so many things for which we are thankful, we should also be helpful. One particular Thanksgiving, one little boy popped up on the front row, and, in a loud voice announced, "Mr. Loaring-Clark, I'm helpful. Every night when I see Daddy coming, I run to Mama and say, 'Shake up the martinis, here comes Daddy.'"

Thomas Quackenboss

We returned to Memphis after living for 10 years in Europe, and did not immediately affiliate with a church. Our life at St. John's began in 1971 when The Rev. Mr. George Calvin Gibson (Mr. Pennepacker's assistant) enlisted me to teach an adult education group. That began a long series of lectures that continued for more than a decade.

I had in mind a survey of Christianity with particular emphasis on Christian roots. The series began with *The Creation of Moral Man,* continued with a two-year study of the *Old Testament* and surrounding cultures, followed with *The Life and Times of Jesus* using the historical viewpoint, and proceeded in an analysis of the Trial of Jesus—the most famous trial in history. After a sabbatical, I taught the Gospels, then a term on *The Acts of the Apostles.*

My forgiving wife Bab accepted the requirement of no social life on Saturday nights while I prepared for Sunday morning's lectures.

Carolyn Comin Forsyth

My fond memories probably start with the years I spent in the children's choir (about 1951-55). Although I have since learned that I can't carry a tune, I loved to sing and sang loudly. Looking back, I marvel that Mr. White never gave me any indication that I didn't make "beautiful music." I remember Mr. White fondly. He was stern during practice, but always had a few jokes and much patience. Our big treat at the end of practice was to sing "There's a Hole in the Bottom of the Sea" that went on for many stanzas and got faster and more lively as it went.

Kay Livingston

When we moved to Memphis from New Orleans, I had heard how unfriendly my new home would be to a girl turning 16. But my first date took me to St. John's to a Y.P.S.L. meeting, and I had a marvelous time. Everyone was so nice. I went to a dance there, then they gave me the lead in a play. I tried to explain that I wasn't a member, but it didn't seem to matter. Except to my family, who were Methodists.

I did not join until after our first child was born, when Tom and I moved to a little house in Normal, close to the church. Our children grew up there, and now are raising more little Episcopalians.

Laura Russell Livingston

Our family joined St. John's in 1933, because Mrs. Harry Ramsay and Mother were girlhood friends.

The Y.P.S.L. met each Sunday evening in the Parish Hall on Buntyn, and Bill Woolwine was an enthusiastic, welcoming president. I recall a 'possum hunt the group enjoyed one year. We went out to the country and, when the dogs treed the 'possum, victory was achieved, we had our weiner roast and sang camp songs.

The choir members teased Mr. Loaring-Clark about his big words in sermons; for example, he said "vicariously speaking." One Sunday the choir bet on his including that expression. He did, and Raynor Allen was so excited, he boomed out in a basso "bingo!"

Helen Freeburg

I well remember going with a friend to Calvary for a Good Friday service when I was about 11, and how much I enjoyed it, even though it was such a solemn occasion. But my family was Presbyterian, and I did not attend St. John's until the summer of 1964. I remember so vividly how much I enjoyed the quiet dignity of the services that summer. I recall how friendly everyone was, and especially how helpful Winnie New and Dorothye Moore were.

In the 1970s I responded to George Gibson's plea and taught seventh grade Sunday School for a year or so. In 1970 I joined the Altar Guild and have found this work to be so rewarding. I am in my third year as a team captain, and am constantly amazed at the beautiful spirit flourishing in this group of women. Needless to say, Penny's gentleness and sense of humor make him a joy to work with.

Nelson joined St. John's in 1978, and his fondness and respect for Penny played the major role in his decision.

I look forward to the utterly lovely ritual when I go to church. Sometimes, one aspect of the service outweighs the others: Richard's music might be especially moving, or Penny's sermon might hit home, or the Eucharist might be more meaningful. But I always get so much out of church.

Connie Austin

John and I were originally communicants of Calvary, but we moved out on Central Avenue about 1934 and started taking Connie and John, Jr. to St. John's. We joined St. John's in 1938.

It was so cold in winter in the old church that our feet nearly froze on the bare wooden floors with cracks in them. Tib used to say, "Some day we'll have a new church and warm feet." In those early days, the church was one long narrow building.

Peggy Perkins and I did the flowers lots of times, and we had fun doing it. Usually the flowers for the altar were brought from someone's garden. Once I found some beautiful brass containers in Chicago, where I was judging a flower show, and bought them for the church. They were used for so many occasions, but I think they were taken during the robbery at the church a few years back.

Tib was very artistic, talented, and versatile. During the church services he would move to the choir stalls where he would sing with the choir, which consisted of about five persons in those early years, then he would move back to the altar and lectern to give the sermon and read the lessons. He would have taken up the offering if necessary. The choir was accompanied by a piano. It was a great day when they graduated to a console organ.

Tib was also a real athlete and sportsman. The gold football on his watch chain impressed the young boys of the parish and provided a ready topic of conversation. He was an avid hunter and was very congenial with the young men at St. John's. He also had a fine rapport with the acolytes. And many people who grew up in St. John's at that time remember badminton games at the rectory.

I always attended the 11:00 o'clock service, but my husband attended the early service every Sunday morning. This was a life-long habit, formed when John was a young acolyte under Bishop Gailor, who was his godfather.

The Bishop promised him a wonderful breakfast at his home every time John served at early service, and that set a precedent that lasted all his life.

Jan. 9, 1949 Bulletin

During 1948, Miss Eleanor Trezevant resurrected used Christmas cards to create more than a thousand cards to send to hospitals, shut-ins, children, and those who needed cheer and brightness.

Elizabeth Boyle

As a small child I went often with my mother to Buntyn to visit her great uncle, Judge John L.T. Sneed, a member of the Tennessee Supreme Court. Part of his house still stands (when this narrative was written in the early 1970s) across the railroad tracks from the Memphis Country Club on Southern Avenue. His wife, Mary Shepherd Sneed, whom we called Aunt Molly, was a devout Episcopalian. I think she grew up in La Grange.

I often played with my sisters in the Sneed orchard, which ran west to Semmes, and I have heard it said in my family, many times, that she gave part of the orchard to the struggling group (Buntyn was at that time a very small group of houses) to build a church on and that they did so and called it St. John's. It was spoken of often, by members of my family, as Aunt Molly's church. The Sneed property, which fronted on Southern and whose western boundary was Semmes, ran all the way back to Spottswood, I believe. I think that the grounds of the old church on Semmes were part of the Sneed property.

Another memory that stands out is that of the Christmas Eve that Dottie Gillespie and I decorated the whole church alone. The entire Altar Guild had planned to decorate for the Christmas services, but it snowed and sleeted the night before and the streets were icy. I couldn't get my car out of the garage, as I had no chains, but Emily Haizlip did have them and came and took me to the church where we found Dottie waiting alone. The church was cold, we had no lunch, but the two of us decorated the entire church and finally managed to get home about dark.

The Rev. Frank T. Donelson, Perpetual Deacon

When Ginger Parker and I married in August 1950, we were probably the second couple to be married in the new church at Central and Greer. The building was not completed. There were concrete floors, brick walls with no plaster and the pews had been made of unseasoned wood.

I assisted Mrs. Norfleet Turner with 10th grade Church School, probably because I was almost six feet tall, and almost as large as most of the boys in the class. I remember a few of them—particularly Richard White's older son, Richard; Ernest Schumacher's son, Mason; and Fred Smith's son, Fred, Jr., presently Chairman of the Board of Fed Ex. They were a rowdy bunch.

I first thought of applying for the Diaconate about 1967. I had been a lay reader. . . and when the assistant minister, a Scotsman named George Thomson, asked if I had any interest in becoming a Deacon, I knew very little about it. But my daughter, Helen, had been seriously ill for a few years and had now regained her health, for which I was most thankful. I felt that I owed something to our church and to the Lord for His help in her recovery. In due course I applied to the Bishop and was accepted for training. I was ordained as Deacon at St. John's on

March 25, 1969, by Bishop Gates, a wonderfully kind man, who became a real friend over the years.

Carrie Sharpe

One time Mr. Irvine Clement, a member of the Bar Association here, gave many books for a library at St. John's. He unloaded them on the floor at one of the back doors. Mr. Parsley called and asked me to get in touch with Paula Shields (who was my friend, in the same chapter with me) and get a library started, since I had studied filing of libraries in a course in college.

The Rev. Jack Bowling

While I was in Memphis (July 1954 to April 1956), I shared my time between St. John's and St. Edward's Mission. It was an honor to be invited to be a full-time Curate at St. John's, and, although I went to the Church of the Advent in Boston instead, I remember it as no better way to begin a ministry. I was ordained a priest in St. John's on the Feast of St. Mark, April 25, 1955, by Bishop Barth.

Louise and I especially remember how wonderful it was to house sit for the Pennepackers in the old Rectory instead of being in our dreadfully hot little apartment.

May Maury Harding

Once when I was in a young women's E.C.W. group, we learned that you cannot expect 10 boxes of frozen peas to get done as quickly as one box does. The Men's Club ate frozen peas without a whimper, and the young women of St. John's learned something about cooking.

Beth Rutland

When Mr. Loaring-Clark died, Mr. Henry Lancaster and his crew stood ready to start digging up the chancel just as soon as permission could be obtained. By 10 in the morning, pile drivers were at work, wheelbarrows of dirt were carried out one by one. The heating of the church building is by radiant heat, with coils winding in and out all under the floor. Each of these pipes had to be tied off before the digging could really start in earnest. It was bitter cold, and we dared not put up the windows as there would be no more heat for some time. As the work progressed, the silt from the concrete gathered. The morning paper had announced that the body would lie in state in the church beginning at 5 o'clock. The workmen started leaving the chancel at 4 o'clock, and the job of cleaning up began. A call was put out to the members to come, bring rags and their vacuum cleaners. So many vacuums were brought that the fuses blew. But every hymn book, prayer book, and pew had to be cleaned—not once, but several times, as the silt kept settling. The cleaning crew was still working at 5 o'clock. As one woman started in to a pew, Mary Robinson handed her a dust rag and asked her to help dust the pew. She replied that she had never been in St. John's before, but she would certainly help.

Eleanor Hussey

I played the piano in the Church School for many years, and was active in a church circle and in the Auxiliary, as it was called at that time, on the Altar Guild and as Flower Chairman. I also played the piano for the monthly service at the Penal Farm for years.

It has been my pleasure to write a short note to accompany the flowers that are sent to the sick each week. Our wonderful flower committee members are: Faye Allen, Blanche Buckingham, Mimi Smith, Connie Austin,

Mary Nelson, Harriett Radcliffe, Flo Pittman Hayes, and Jane Holmgrain.

Tom and Sherry Prewitt

Tom: There was a great deal of comradeship among the kids that I grew up with and went to Church School with and played basketball and baseball with at St. John's. I was born and baptised into St. John's. It's a place that shared in my youth and my strivings toward maturity. Now that I'm married and have a family, I consider it a very integral part of the rearing of my two sons.

Sherry: I came to St. John's when I married Tom. But I believe that when families bring their children to church and have them grow up in an atmosphere of the caring and warmth of being around children they know, that often forms lifelong friendships.

Sandra Freund

Don, our children, and I were communicants of Barth House when Jack Abell approached me in 1978 about having an Orff Choir program for the children at St. John's, as I had been doing for three years at Ascension Lutheran Church. We created the choir in 1980.

Margaret Huntzicker

I must have been about 16 years old when I joined the adult choir. At that time all the girls were painting their toenails, which my father told me was considered a very bad thing to do and that he did not approve. One Sunday I painted my toenails (everybody has to do something stupid once in a while), put on brand new white linen sandals, and rushed into my vestments. The choir mother, a Mrs. Adams, was big and stern. She said, "Where are your hose?" I said I am not wearing any. She said, "Who told you you could sing in this choir with painted toenails?" I said, "No one," and you could hear a pin drop in the choir room. She said, "You are not singing in my choir with painted toenails on Sunday morning." So I immediately went out, crying, and got Mr. Loaring-Clark. He said, "Margaret, she runs the choir; I don't. You have got to obey her wishes." Then I went to Mrs. Beasley. She wholeheartedly agreed it was in very poor taste and that from now on I should not paint my toenails and should wear hose. That's when some of the men in the choir nicknamed me "the Imp."

Fred Northup

When I was graduated from seminary in 1973, Bishop Vander Horst assigned me to St. John's Church. I remember particularly the weekly Tuesday evening planning meeting for the "Contemporary Service." Each week Grayson Smith, Dot Davis, three to ten others and I would meet at great length to plan that service. The service itself was a great joy to me and the faithful who gathered Sunday mornings at 8:30. We were able to explore in quite different ways many of the themes and issues of that time. One time we recorded Eugart Yerian's voice—with reverberation—as God's, and then played it at the appropriate moment in the service. Once Terry Holmes, then Dean of the Seminary at Sewanee, was present and Joe Alford, who later went to seminary, had arranged for a "guard," who, bearing a double-barrelled shotgun, led a group of "prisoners" into the church, had them seated among surprised and uncertain worshippers, then stood watch from the pulpit.

In the spring and in the fall of both years that I served

at St. John's, we planned what we called a "Getaway." The first was held at Pickwick Landing State Park and the last three at Reelfoot State Park. For each of these weekends, 35-50 adults explored a different dimension of their lives and faith.

The Rev. H. Gordon Bernard

In the spring of 1959 when the deadline came and all the Tennessee seminarians were waiting as the post office opened, the letter from Bishop Barth assigned me as assistant to St. John's. Most of the people I asked about the church told me about the murals. Jayne and I were prepared for Byzantine murals in a Williamsburg church, but when we came to the church on June 15 we were not prepared to be overwhelmed by its beauty. We were warmly welcomed.

I began to learn something of what it meant to be a priest, and no one could have been more fortunate in his mentor. Penny's patience with my foul-ups made me work harder. The happy occasion of my ordination to the Priesthood three years later, the gift of the new car from the Men's Club, all the efforts to see to our comfort and well-being were a reflection of the wonderful friends we found there. When the time of leaving came in 1962, it was a hard decision to move to St. Luke's, Cleveland, Tennessee. But the time had come to put into practice what Penny had taught me by word and example.

Dr. and Mrs. Duane Carr

Orange Mound Day Nursery Board of Directors

*Erna Bladow (right) and
Melda McDonald*

The Rev. Mr. Loaring-Clark had hoped the church would have a school — which did occur temporarily.
It was under the direction of Mahaffey White and Frances Coe.

Harry A. Ramsey, Senior Warden

Samuel Carey

Leaders

Appendix 2

Vicars and Rectors

Dr. Charles Stewart	1889-1891
The Rev. Mr. Peter Wager	1871-73, 1897-1913
The Rev. Mr. Grant Knoft	1916-1918 ?
The Rev. Dr. Manville(?) Bennett	1919
The Rev. Mr. Paul N. Williams	Fall, 1919-1922
The Rev. Mr. Martin Luther Tate, rector of Holy Trinity Church, served 2 congregations	1922-1926
The Rev. Mr. Alfred Loaring-Clark	1928-1952
The Rev. Mr. Wallace M. Pennepacker	1952-1983
The Rev. Mr. Stuart Wood	1984-1988
The Rev. Dr. James M. Coleman	1988-1993
The Rev. Mr. L. Noland Pipes, Jr.	1994-

Associate Rectors

The Rev. Mr. Henry Nutt Parsley
The Rev. Mr. Wallace M. Pennepacker
The Rev. Mr. Arthur Fippinger
The Rev. Mr. Jack Bowling
The Rev. Mr. Gordon Bernard
The Rev. Mr. George Thomson
The Rev. Mr. Carter Gregory
The Rev. Mr. George Calvin Gibson
The Rev. Mr. Frederick B. Northup
The Rev. Mr. Noble R. Walker
The Rev. Mr. Marshall S. Scott
The Rev. Mr. Lewis McKee
The Rev. Mrs. Iris Slocum
The Rev. Mr. Joseph N. Davis
The Rev. Mr. Myron Manasterski

Ordinations in St. John's

William Augustus Jones, Jr.	Deacon, 1952
Frank Mauldin McClain	Deacon, 1952
Urbin Albert Brown	Deacon, 1952
John Greening (Jack) Arthur	Deacon, 1952
Herbert Pendleton Jordan	Deacon, 1952
Jack Denver Bowling	Priest, 1955
Hal Gordon Bernard	Priest, 1960
Benjamin Harrison Shawhan	Deacon, 1960
James Dabney Curtis	Deacon, 1964
Craig Walter Casey	Deacon, 1964
Frank Taylor Donelson, Jr.	Deacon, 1969
Frederick Bowen Northup	Priest, 1974
Joseph Stanley Trowbridge Alford	Deacon, 1978
Marshall Stuart Scott	Priest, 1981
George Maclin Klee	Deacon, 1984
Battle Alexander Beasley	Deacon, 1986
Thomas Scholfield Hotchkiss	Deacon, 1993
James M. Guill	Deacon, 1996

Organists of St. John's

James E. Morrison	1929-1930
Carolyn "Ursi" McGinley	1930-1946
Fergus O'Conner	1946-1950
Vernon Perdue Davis	(Briefly between 1948-49)
Richard T. White	1950-1986
John P. Ayer, Jr.	1986-

Vestry

(Early records are incomplete)

1928   First Vestry of the current St. John's Parish:

        H. A. Ramsay
        Palmer Farnsworth
        T. K. Robinson, Sr.
        C. B. Rutledge
        Walter E. Lott
        B. H. Shawhan
        John T. Tyler
        L. M. Woolwine
        Charles Burch

W. G. Abbott
Nathan Acree
Thomas C. Adams
Mark Adkins
Frank Ahlgren
A. Calloway Allen
W. Harwell Allen
Harwell Allen, Jr.
John Allen
Raynor Allen
Granville Allison
Dr. W. D. Anderson
Mrs. Richard Ashley
Mrs. Malcolm Aste
Don Austin
McNeill Ayres
Mrs. Hal P. Bailey, Jr.
John Barbee

Joe Barnwell
Jack Barton
Dr. Billy Rogers Beasley
Shubael T. Beasley
William Belcher
M. O. Bennett
James R. Bettendorf
Julian Bondurant
Casey Bowlin
A. B. Bowman
Bayard Boyle
Mrs. William Brooks
Mrs. James Brown
William R. Bruce, Jr.
Beverly Buckingham
Jack Bugbee
Judge Charles N. Burch
James Burton

Paul Calame
Paul Calame, Jr.
Patrick Carey
Mrs. Patrick Carey
Sam D. Carey
Dr. Duane M. Carr
Oscar Carr
Mrs. E. Alan Catmur
John Catmur
John Cawthon
Ross B. Clark
Ross B. Clark, II
Sam Cole, Jr.
Mrs. Sam Cole, Jr.
M. S. Cone
Fowler Cooper
Joe Craig
Dr. Thurman Crawford
Mrs. Roy F. Creson, Jr.
Roy F. Creson, Jr.
Edward I. Curry, III
Dana C. Curtis, Jr.
James L. Dallas
Jane Darr Orvis
Carl Davis
Mrs. Carl Davis
J. E. Denham
Dr. Richard DeSaussure
Ed Dewey
Mrs. John Dillon
Frank T. Donelson, Jr.
Kenneth Duncan
Dr. C. H. Eades, Jr.

Dr. C. L. Eades
Goodloe Early, Jr.
Mrs. Goodloe Early, Jr.
W. T. Edge, Jr.
Palmer Farnsworth
Minter Farnsworth
Mrs. William Fay
Foster Fitzhugh
Mrs. William Flowers
William Flowers
W. L. Ford, Jr.
Dr. David Fox
Mrs. David Fox
E. B. Fox
Mrs. Charles Freeburg
Mrs. Nelson Freeburg
Philip Freeburg
Mrs. Donald Freund
Dan Fulton
Dr. Eugene Gadberry
Tom Garrison
John V. M. (Jack) Gibson
P. H. Giddeon
William Gillaspie
Paul Gillespie
Trow Gillespie
Russell Gregg
Henry Haizlip, Jr.
Mrs. Henry Haizlip, Jr.
Roy Hancock
Mrs. Haywood Henderson
Dr. J. P. Henry
Dr. T. S. Hill

Bruce Hillyer
G. Benton Holmgrain
Ronald Hopton
W. F. Hughes
Mrs. Herbert Humphreys
Herbert Humphreys
Oscar Hurt
J. L. Hutter, Jr.
Oliver Jeanes
Hall Jones
Herbert Jordan
Douglas Kelso
D. T. Kimbrough
Dr. Charles King
David King
H. W. Lancaster
L. S. Lawo, Jr.
Ralph Lewis
Thomas Livingston
Mrs. William G. Logan
William G. Logan
Walter E. Lott
H. S. McCleskey
C. N. McConnell
E. N. McConnell
James McGehee
Forrest McGinley
E. P. McNeil
F. Allan Mackenzie
Richard Magevney
Lauch Magruder
William Marty
Mrs. R. A. Mayhall

R. Arthur Mayhall
Joseph H. Miller, Jr.
Mrs. Joseph H. Miller, Jr.
Lucy Miller Craven
Karl Moore
Mrs. Thomas Moore
Henry Morgan
Seldon Murray
James Napier, Jr.
Kenneth Nathan
William Nelson
Robert Nesbit
Edward H. Newell
W. L. Nichol
W. Lytle Nichol, IV
Mrs. W. Lytle Nichol, IV
Fred M. Niell
Gilbert Palmer, Jr.
Mrs. M. B. Parker, Jr.
Malcolm Parker
Mrs. John Peeples
John Pepper
Allen W. Phelps
Alfred Pittman
John G. Powell
Julie Powell
Julian Prewitt
Thomas R. Prewitt
Marion Price
Ronald Prothero
Mrs. Ronald Prothero
J. Seth Pund
Thomas Quackenboss

James C. Rainer, III
H. A. Ramsay
H. A. Ramsay, Jr.
Alan Rankine
E. T. Reece
Dr. Richard J. Reynolds, Jr.
Charles D. Richardson, Jr.
Gibson Riley
Ronald Robertson
T. K. Robinson
Richard Rodenbaugh
Pat Rohrbacher
Charles A. Rond
William F. Ross
Blake N. Russell
James F. Russell
J. K. Rutland, Jr.
C. B. Rutledge
E. P. Schumacher
Benjamin H. Shawhan
James Shields
Eulyse Smith
Grayson Smith
Jay Smith
Joseph Snider
Leo Soroha
Matthew Spinolo
Phillip Stevenson
Dr. Marcus Stewart
John Stout
Judy Sullivan
Dr. W. D. Sutliff
Mrs. W. D. Sutliff

Fitzhugh Taylor, Jr.
Mrs. Fitzhugh Taylor
James A. Taylor
William H. Terry
Thomas Thayer
George R. Thompson
Norfleet Turner
Burnet Tuthill
John T. Tyler
Herbert Vaiden
J. Leonard Vaiden
Philip Vaiden
Robert Van Doren
Victor Vescovo
Dr. W. J. von Lackum
J. Richard Walker
Judge Phil Wallace
William T. Whitley
Christopher Williams, Jr.
David Williams
Oscar Williams
Judd Williford
Lloyd Winters
L. M. Woolwine
David Work
Harry Work
Eugart Yerian

**Presidents,
St. John's Episcopal
Churchwomen**

Mrs. Palmer Farnsworth
Mrs. T. K. Robinson, Sr.
Mrs. Harry A. Ramsay, Sr.
Mrs. Joe R. Craig
Mrs. W. L. Nichol
Mrs. Charles N. Burch
Mrs. M. O. Bennett
Mrs. Sam Carey
Mrs. Shubael T. Beasley
Mrs. Russell Gregg
Mrs. Clarence Saunders
Mrs. Lucian Dent
Mrs. Ernest Kelly
Mrs. Ronald Hopton
Mrs. W. L. Ford, Jr.
Mrs. Herbert Vaiden
Mrs. W. Vincent Beal
Mrs. T. S. Hill
Mrs. W. J. Bunn
Mrs. Harry H. Work, Jr.
Mrs. Edwin Clifford Jeffries
Mrs. Malcolm B. Parker, Jr.
Mrs. Thomas D. Moore
Mrs. William H. L. Kitts
Mrs. James C. Rainer, III
Mrs. David B. Fox
Mrs. William Flowers
Mrs. Eugart Yerian
Mrs. Richard J. Reynolds, Jr.
Mrs. Joseph H. Miller, Jr.

Mrs. E. Alan Catmur
Mrs. Harry A. Ramsay, Jr.
Mrs. Roy F. Creson, Jr.
Mrs. W. Seldon Murray, III
Mrs. John R. Cawthon
Mrs. Reba Hemphill
Mrs. Fred M. Niell, Sr.
Mrs. Harry H. Wilcox, Jr.
Mrs. Clark Taylor
Mrs. Kutcher Threefoot
Mrs. Eugene E. Garrety
Mrs. G. Goodloe Early
Mrs. James D. Gordon
Mrs. Philip M. Lewis
Mrs. Eugene Pearson
Mrs. James R. Bettendorf
Mrs. William G.
Pennepacker
Mrs. Karl Moore

Woodcut by Mahaffey White

Sources Consulted

In addition to vestry minutes, annual reports, correspondence, minutes from the Women's Auxiliary (and succeeding organizations with different names), Church School roll books, scrapbooks, bulletins, and various publications by St. John's, other sources included Diocesan reports and journals, local newspapers, indices, Trust Deeds in Shelby County Register's office, and reference books. Newspapers were scanned selectively for the years 1832 to 1900. The listing for newspapers included many that were published for brief periods.

The American Eagle
Appeal-Avalanche
Argus
The Commercial Appeal
The Avalanche
The Daily Appeal
The Daily Eagle
The Daily Eagle & Enquirer
The Daily Enquirer
The Daily Public Ledger
Memphis Daily Appeal
The Memphis Daily Bulletin
The Memphis Daily Commercial
Memphis Evening Herald
The Memphis Press-Scimitar
The Randolph Recorder
The Weekly Appeal
The Weekly Public Ledger
The Whig

Bruton Parish Churchyard and Church. Williamsburg, VA: Bruton Parish Church, 1976.

Coppock, Paul R. *Memphis Sketches*. Memphis: Friends of Memphis and Shelby County Libraries, 1976.

Davies-Rodgers, Ellen. *The Romance of the Episcopal Church in West Tennessee, 1832-1964*. Memphis: The Plantation Press, 1964.

Davies-Rodgers, Ellen. *The Holy Innocents*. Memphis: The Plantation Press, 1965.

Davies-Rodgers, Ellen. *The Great Book, Calvary Protestant Episcopal Church, 1832-1972*. Memphis: The Plantation Press, 1973.

Davies-Rodgers, Ellen. *Heirs Through Hope, The Episcopal Diocese of West Tennessee*. Memphis: The Plantation Press, 1983.

Dent, Phoebe. *The Murals of St. John's Episcopal Church*. Unpublished.

Falk, Peter Hastings. *Who Was Who in American Art*. Madison, CT: Sound View Press, 1985.

Ferguson, George. *Signs & Symbols in Christian Art*. NY: Oxford University Press, 1955.

Harding, May Maury. *The Murals of St. John's Episcopal Church*. Unpublished.

Mathes, J. Harvey. *Old Guard in Gray*. Memphis: Press of S.C. Toof & Co., 1897.

Memphis as She Is. Memphis, Pittsburgh and London: Historical and Descriptive Publishing Company, 1887.

Morris, Richard B., Ed. *Encyclopedia of American History*. NY: Harper & Brothers, 1953.

Nazor, Mary Louise Graham. *Gravestone Inscriptions from Shelby County, TN Cemeteries*, Vol. III, Part 2. Memphis: Tennessee Genealogical Society, 1995.

Quinn, Rev. D.A. *Heroes and Heroines of Memphis*. Providence, RI: E. L. Freeman & Son, 1887.

Rainey's Memphis City Directory. 1855-68.

Seymour, Charles M., Ed. *St. John's Church, Knoxville, 1846-1946*. Knoxville, TN: Published by the Vestry of St. John's Parish, 1947.

Sister Hughetta's Reminiscences. Unpublished.

Taylor, David Fox. *Twentieth Century Church Decoration and the Contribution of John H. deRosen*. Thesis submitted to the Department of Art and Archeology of Princeton University, 1957.

Tilly, Bette B., with Pat Faudree and Bettie Shenk. *A Visit to Buntyn*. Memphis: MIFA, 1979.

Tennessee Records of Shelby County, Minute Book No. 1, 1850-1859. Historical Records Project, Copied under Works Progress Administration, 1938.

The War of the Rebellion, A Compilation of the Official Records of the Union and Confederate Armies. Washington, DC: Government Printing Office, 1901.

Vedder, O.F. *History of the City of Memphis and Shelby County Tennessee*. Syracuse, NY: D. Mason & Co, 1888.

Weir, M. Harris. *Religious Institutions and Structures, Shelby County*. Federal Writers' Project for Tennessee State Guide.

Wingfield, Marshall. *Literary Memphis*. Memphis: The West Tennessee Historical Society, 1942.

Wrenn, Lynette Bony. *Taxing District of Shelby County, A Political and Administrative History of Memphis, TN, 1879-1893*. Dissertation, 1983.

Photos on pages 17 and 18 by Dave Darnell, courtesy *The Commercial Appeal*.

Color photos of murals by Hud Andrews.

"Bless, we beseech Thee, O Heavenly Father, the clergy, the staff, and the members of this parish with an ever-growing vision of the Christ in His beauty; that in the strength of that vision we may labor together, ever in unity and in love, without haste but without ceasing, for the extension of Thy Kingdom, through Jesus Christ our Lord. Amen."

Written by The Rev. Mr. Loaring-Clark and used every Sunday at the Altar by him and later by The Rev. Mr. Pennepacker until the 1979 Book of Common Prayer was published.

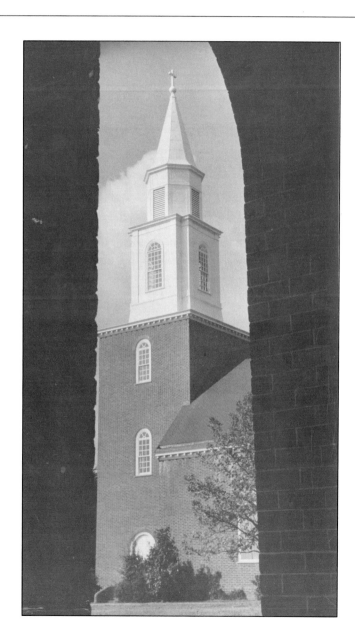